Harry Castlemon

The Sportsman's Club Afloat

Harry Castlemon

The Sportsman's Club Afloat

ISBN/EAN: 9783742898692

Manufactured in Europe, USA, Canada, Australia, Japa

Cover: Foto ©ninafisch / pixelio.de

Manufactured and distributed by brebook publishing software (www.brebook.com)

Harry Castlemon

The Sportsman's Club Afloat

CHAPTER I.
On the Gulf again . . . . Page 5

CHAPTER II.
A Surprise 25

CHAPTER III.
Outwitted 45

CHAPTER IV.
Fairly afloat 66

CHAPTER V.
The Deserters 88

CHAPTER VI.
A Chapter of Incidents 111

CHAPTER VII.
Don Casper 129

CHAPTER VIII.
Chase rises to explain 143

CHAPTER IX.
Wilson runs a race 164

CONTENTS.

CHAPTER X.
A Lucky Fall . . . . Page 181

CHAPTER XI.
"Sheep Ahoy!" 198

CHAPTER XII.
The Banner under fire 214

CHAPTER XIII.
The Spanish Frigate 231

CHAPTER XIV.
The Yacht Lookout 254

SPORTSMAN'S CLUB AFLOAT.

CHAPTER I.

ON THE GULF AGAIN.

"I ASSURE you, gentlemen, that you do not regret this mistake more than I do. I would not have had it happen for anything."

It was the captain of the revenue cutter who spoke. He, with Walter Gaylord, Mr. Craven, Mr. Chase and the collector of the port, was standing on the wharf, having just returned with his late prisoners from the custom-house, whither the young captain of the Banner had been to provide himself with clearance papers. The latter had narrated as much of the history of Fred Craven's adventures, which we have attempted to describe in the first volume of this series, as he was acquainted with, and the recital had thrown the revenue captain into a state of great excitement. The yacht was anchored in the harbor, a short distance astern of the cutter, and alongside the wharf lay the only tug of which the village could boast, the John Basset, which Mr. Chase and Mr. Craven had hired to carry them to Lost Island in pursuit of the smugglers.

"There must be some mistake about it," continued the captain of the cutter. "A boy captured by a gang of smugglers and carried to sea in a dug-out! I never heard of such a thing before. I know you gentlemen will pardon me for what I have done, even though you may think me to have been over-zealous in the discharge of my duty. Your yacht corresponds exactly with the description given me of the smuggler."

"You certainly made a great blunder," said Mr. Craven, who was in very bad humor; "and there is no knowing what it may cost us."

"But you can make some amends for it by starting for Lost Island at once," said Mr. Chase. "You will find two of the smugglers there, and perhaps you can compel them to tell you something of the vessel of which you are in search. More than that, they have made a prisoner of my son, and he knows what has become of Fred Craven."

"I am at your service. I will sail again immediately, and I shall reach the island about daylight. If you gentlemen with your tug arrive there before I do and need assistance, wait until I come. Captain Gaylord, if you will step into my gig I shall be happy to take you on board your vessel. You may go home now, and these gentlemen and myself will attend to those fellows out there on Lost Island. If we find them we shall certainly capture them."

"And when you do that, I shall not be far away," replied Walter.

"Why, you are not going to venture out in this wind again with that cockle-shell, are you?" asked the captain, in surprise.

"I am, sir. I built the Banner, and I know what she can do. She has weathered the Gulf breeze once to-night, and she can do it again. I am not going home until I see Fred Craven safe out of his trouble. In order to find out where he is, I must have an interview with Henry Chase."

Mr. Craven and Mr. Chase, who were impatient to start for Lost Island again, walked off toward the tug, and Walter stepped down into the captain's gig and was carried on board the Banner. His feelings as he sprang on the deck of his vessel were very different from those he had experienced when he left her. The last time he clambered over her rail he was a prisoner, guarded by armed men and charged with one of the highest crimes known to the law. Now he was free again, the Banner was all his own, and he was at liberty to go where he pleased.

"Mr. Butler, send all the cutter's hands into the gig," said the revenue captain, as he sprang on board the yacht.

"Very good, sir," replied the lieutenant. "Pass the word for all the prize crew to muster on the quarter-deck."

"Banner's men, ahoy!" shouted Walter, thrusting his head down the companion-way. "Up you come with a jump. Perk, get under way immediately."

For a few seconds confusion reigned supreme on board the yacht. The revenue men who had been lying about the deck came aft in a body; those who had been guarding the prisoners in the cabin tumbled up the ladder, closely followed by the boy crew, who, delighted to find themselves once more at liberty, shouted and hurrahed until they were hoarse.

"All hands stand by the capstan!" yelled Perk.

"Never mind the anchor," said Walter. "Get to sea at once."

"Eugene, slip the chain," shouted Perk. "Stand by the halliards fore and aft."

"Hold on a minute, captain," exclaimed the master of the cutter, who had been extremely polite and even cringing ever since he learned that the boys who had been his prisoners were the sons of the wealthiest and most influential men about Bellville. "I should like an opportunity to muster my crew, if you please."

"Can you not do that on board your own vessel?" asked Walter.

"I might under ordinary circumstances, but of late my men have been seizing every opportunity to leave me, and I am obliged to watch them very closely. They have somehow learned that a Cuban privateer, which has escaped from New York, is lying off Havana waiting for a crew, and they are deserting me by dozens. There may be some deserters stowed away about this yacht, for all I know."

"Never mind," replied Walter, who was so impatient to get under way that he could think of nothing else. "If there are, I will return them to you when I meet you at Lost Island. Good-bye, captain, and if you see me on the Gulf again don't forget that I have papers now."

By this time the Banner was fairly under sail. Perk saw that the revenue men were still on board, and knew that they would have some difficulty in getting into their boat when the yacht was scudding down the harbor at the rate of eight knots an hour, but that made no difference to him. His commander had ordered him to get under way, and he did it without the loss of a moment. He slipped the anchor, hoisted the same sails the Banner had carried when battling with the Gulf breeze three hours before, and in a few seconds more was dragging the revenue gig through the water at a faster rate than she had ever travelled before. Her crew tumbled over the rail one after another, and when they were all in the boat Bab cast off the painter, and the Banner sped on her way, leaving the gig behind.

"What was the matter, Walter? did they really take us for smugglers?" asked the Club in concert, as they gathered about the young captain. "What did you tell them; and has anything new happened that you are going to sea again in such a hurry?"

"Ask your questions one at a time and they will last longer," replied Walter; who then proceeded in a very few words to explain matters. The captain of the cutter had really been stupid enough to believe that the Banner was a smuggler, he said, and so certain was he of the fact that he would listen to no explanation. Mr. Craven had told him the story of the two smugglers who had taken a prisoner to Lost Island, but the revenue commander would not believe a word of it, and persisted in his determination to take his captives to the village. When they arrived there and the collector of the port had been called up, of course the matter was quickly settled, and then the captain appeared to be very sorry for what he had done, and was as plausible and fawning as he had before been insolent and overbearing. Pierre and his father would certainly be captured now, for Mr. Chase and Mr. Craven had chartered the John Bassett to carry them to Lost Island, and the revenue captain would also sail at once and render all the assistance in his power.

"Humph!" exclaimed Eugene, when Walter

finished his story, "We don't want any of his help, or the tug's either. Crack on, Walter, and let's reach the island and have the work over before they get there."

"That would be useless," answered the cautious young captain. "The Banner's got as much as she can carry already; and besides we can't expect to compete with a tug or a vessel of the size of the cutter. If we reach the island in time to see Chase rescued, I shall be satisfied. If any of you are in want of sleep you may go below, and Bab and I will manage the yacht."

But none of the Club felt the need of rest just then. Things were getting too exciting. With a couple of smugglers before them to be captured, two swift rival pursuers behind, to say nothing of the gale and the waves which tossed the staunch little Banner about like a nut-shell, and the intense impatience and anxiety they felt to learn something of the situation of the missing secretary—under circumstances like these sleep was not to be thought of. They spent the next half hour in discussing the exciting adventures that had befallen them since their encounter with Bayard Bell and his crowd, and then Eugene, after sundry emphatic injunctions from his brother to keep his weather eye open and mind what he was about, took Perk's place at the wheel, while the latter, who always acted as ship's cook in the absence of Sam the negro, went below to prepare the eatables which Walter had provided before leaving home. The baskets containing the provisions had been taken into the galley. In the floor of this galley was a small hatchway leading into the hold where the water-butts, fuel for the stove, tool-chests, ballast, and extra rigging were stowed away; and when Perk approached the galley from the cabin he was surprised to see that the hatchway was open, and that a faint light, like that emitted by a match, was shining through it from below.

The sight was a most unexpected one, and for an instant Perk stood paralyzed with alarm. His face grew as pale as death, and his heart seemed to stop beating. Who had been careless enough to open that hatch and go into the hold with an uncovered light? Eugene of course—he was always doing something he had no business to do—and he had set fire to some of the combustible matter there. Perk had often heard Uncle Dick tell how it felt to have one's vessel burned under him, and shuddering at the recital, had hoped most fervently that he might never know the feeling by experience But now he was in a fair way to learn all about it. Already he imagined the Banner a charred and smoking wreck, and he and his companions tossing about on the waves clinging to spars and life-buoys. These thoughts passed through Perk's mind in one second of time; then recovering the use of his legs and his tongue, he sprang forward and shouted out one word which rang through the cabin, and fell with startling distinctness upon the ears of the watchful crew on deck.

"Fire!" yelled Perk, with all the power of his lungs.

That was all he said, but it was enough to strike terror to the heart of every one of the boy sailors who heard it. Somebody else heard it too—some persons who did not belong to the Banner, and who had no business on board of her. Perk did not know it then, but he found it out a moment afterwards when he entered the galley, for, just as he seized the hatch, intending to close the opening that led into the hold and thus shut out the draft, a grizzly head suddenly appeared from below, one brawny hand holding a hatchet, was placed upon the combings, and the other was raised to prevent the descent of the hatch.

If it is possible for a boy to see four things at once, to come to a conclusion on four different points, to act, and to do it all in less than half a second of time, Perk certainly performed the feat. He saw that the man who so suddenly made his appearance in the hatchway was dressed in the uniform of the revenue service; that he had a companion in the hold; that the latter was in the act of taking an adze from the tool-chest; and that he held in his hand a smoky lantern which gave out the faint, flickering light that shone through the hatchway.

When the boy had noted these things, some scraps of the conversation he had overheard between Walter and the revenue captain came into his mind. These men were deserters from the cutter, and he had discovered them just in time to prevent mischief. They were preparing to make an immediate attack upon the Banner's crew, and had provided themselves with weapons to overcome any opposition they might meet. If they were allowed to come on deck they would take the vessel out of the hands of her crew, and shape her course toward

Havana, where the Cuban privateer was supposed to be lying. Perk did not object to the men joining the privateer if they felt so inclined—that was the revenue captain's business, and not his—but he was determined that they should not assume control of the Banner, and take her so far into the Gulf in such a gale if he could prevent it.

"Avast, there!" exclaimed the sailor, in a savage tone of voice, placing his hand against the hatch to keep Perk from slamming it down on his head. "We want to come up."

"But I want you to stay down," replied the boy; "and we'll see who will have his way."

The sailor made an upward spring, and Perk flung down the hatchway at the same moment, throwing all his weight upon it as he did so. The result was a collision between the man's head and the planks of which the hatchway was composed, the head getting the worst of it. The deserter was knocked over on the opposite side of the opening and caught and held as if he had been in a vise, his breast being pressed against the combings, and the sharp corner of the hatch, with Perk's one hundred and forty pounds on top of it, falling across his shoulders.

"Now just listen to me a minute, and I'll tell you what's a fact," said the boy, who, finding that the enemy was secured beyond all possibility of escape, began to recover his usual coolness and courage; "I've got you."

"But you had better let me go mighty sudden," replied the sailor, struggling desperately to seize Perk over his shoulder. "Push up the hatch, Tom," he added, addressing his confederate below.

All these events, which we have been so long in narrating, occupied scarcely a minute in taking place. Walter sprang toward the companion-way the instant Perk's wild cry fell upon his ears, and pale and breathless burst into the cabin, followed by Bab and Wilson. When he opened the door he discovered Perk in the position we have described. A single glance at the uniform worn by the man whose head and shoulders were protruding from the hatchway, was enough to explain everything.

"Now, here's a go!" exclaimed Bab, in great amazement.

"Yes; and there'll be a worse go than this if you don't let me out," replied the prisoner, savagely. "Push up the hatch, Tom."

"The revenue captain was right in his suspicions
2

after all, wasn't he?" said Walter, as he and Wilson advanced and wrested the hatchet from the sailor's hand. "I don't think that your attempt to reach Cuba will be very successful, my friend."

"That remains to be seen. Push up the hatch, Tom. If I once get on deck I'll make a scattering among these young sea monkeys. Push up the hatch, I tell you."

This was the very thing the man below had been trying to do from the first, but without success. The hatchway was small, and was so nearly filled by the body of the prisoner, who was a burly fellow, that his companion in the hold had no chance to exert his strength. He could not place his shoulders against the hatch, and there was no handspike in the hold, or even a billet of wood strong enough to lift with. He breathed hard and uttered a good many threats, but accomplished nothing.

"I wish now I had given that captain time to muster his men," said Walter. "This fellow is a deserter from the cutter, of course; but he shall never go to Havana in our yacht. Bab, go on deck and bring down three handspikes."

Bab disappeared, and when he returned with the

implements, Walter took one and handed Wilson another.

"Now, Perk," continued the young captain, "take a little of your weight off the hatch and let that man go back into the hold. We'd rather have him down there than up here."

"I know it," said Perk. "But just listen to me, and I'll tell you what's a fact: Perhaps he won't go back."

"I think he will," answered Walter, in a very significant tone of voice. "He'd rather go back of his own free will than be knocked back. Try him and see."

Perk got off the hatch, and the sailor, after taking a look at the handspikes that were flourished over his head, slid back into the hold without uttering a word; while Bab, hardly waiting until his head was below the combings, slammed down the hatch, threw the bar over it and confined it with a padlock. This done, the four boys stood looking at one another with blanched cheeks.

"Where's the fire, Perk?" asked Walter.

"There is none, I am glad to say. The light I saw shining from the hold came from a lantern that those fellows have somehow got into their possession."

"Well, I'd rather fight the deserters than take my chances with a fire if it was once fairly started," replied Walter, much relieved. "How many of them are there?"

"Only two that I saw. But they can do a great deal of mischief if they feel in the humor for it."

"That is just what I was thinking of," chimed in Bab. "You take it very coolly, Walter. Don't you know that if they get desperate they can set fire to the yacht, or bore through the bottom and sink her?"

"I thought of all that before we drove that man back there; but what else could we have done? If we had brought him up here to tie him, he would have attacked us as soon as he touched the deck, and engaged our attention until his companion could come to his assistance. Perk, you and Wilson stay down here and guard that hatch. Call me if you hear anything."

"I hear something now," said Wilson.

"So do I," exclaimed Perk. "I hear those fellows swearing and storming about in the hold; but they won't get out that way, I guess."

Walter and Bab returned to the deck and found Eugene in a high state of excitement, and impatient to hear all about the fire. He was much relieved, although his excitement did not in the least abate, to learn that the danger that had threatened the yacht was of an entirely different character, and that by Perk's prompt action it had been averted, at least for the present. Of course he could not stay on deck after so thrilling a scene had been enacted below. He gave the wheel into his brother's hands, and went down into the galley to see how things looked there. He listened in great amazement to Perk's account of the affair, and placed his ear at the hatch in the hope of hearing something that would tell him what the prisoners were about. But all was silent below. The deserters had ceased their swearing and threatening, and were no doubt trying to decide what they should do next.

The crew of the yacht were not nearly so confidant and jubilant as they had been before this incident happened, and nothing more was said about the lunch. The presence of two desperate characters on board their vessel was enough to awaken the most serious apprehensions in their minds. During the rest of the voyage they were on the alert to check any attempt at escape on the part of the prisoners, and those on deck caught up handspikes and rushed down into the cabin at every unusual sound. But the journey was accomplished without any mishap, and finally the bluffs on Lost Island began to loom up through the darkness. After sailing around the island without discovering any signs of the smugglers, the Banner came about, and running before the wind like a frightened deer, held for the cove into which Chase and his captors had gone with the pirogue a few hours before. The young captain, with his speaking-trumpet in his hand, stood upon the rail, the halliards were manned fore and aft, and the careful Bab sent to the wheel. These precautions were taken because the Banner was now about to perform the most dangerous part of her voyage to the island. The entrance to the cove was narrow, and the cove itself extended but a short distance inland, so that if the yacht's speed were not checked at the proper moment, the force with which she was driven by the gale, would send her high and dry upon the beach.

The little vessel flew along with the speed of an arrow, seemingly on the point of dashing herself in pieces on the rocks, against which the surf beat with a roar like that of a dozen cannon; but, under the skilful management of her young captain, doubled the projecting point in safety, and was carried on the top of a huge wave into the still waters of the cove. Now was the critical moment, and had Walter been up and doing he might have saved the Banner from the catastrophe which followed. But he did not give an order, and it is more than likely that he would not have been obeyed if he had. He and his crew stood rooted to the deck, bewildered by the scene that burst upon their view. A bright fire was roaring and crackling on the beach, and by the aid of the light it threw out, every object in the cove could be distinguished. The first thing the crew of the Banner noticed was a small schooner moored directly in their path—the identical one they had seen loading at Bellville; the second, a group of men, one of whom they recognised, standing on the beach; and the third, a cave high up the bluff, in the mouth of which stood one of the boys of whom they were in search, Henry Chase, whose face was white with excitement and terror. He was throwing his arms wildly about his head, and shouting at the top of his voice.

"Banner ahoy!" he yelled.

"Hallo!" replied Walter, as soon as he found his tongue.

"Get away from here!" shouted Chase. "Get away while you can. That vessel is the smuggler, and Fred Craven is a prisoner on board of her."

But it was too late for the yacht to retreat. Before Walter could open his mouth she struck the smuggling vessel with a force sufficient to knock all the boy crew off their feet, breaking the latter's bowsprit short off, and then swung around with her stern in the bushes, where she remained wedged fast, with her sails shaking in the wind.

CHAPTER II.

A SURPRISE.

THE last time we saw Henry Chase he was sitting in the mouth of "The Kitchen"—that was the name given to the cave in which he had taken refuge after destroying the pirogue—with his axe in his hand, waiting to see what Coulte and Pierre, who had just disappeared down the gully, were going to do next. He had been holding a parley with his captors, and they, finding that he had fairly turned the tables on them, and that he was not to be frightened into surrendering himself into their hands again, had gone off to talk the matter over and decide upon some plan to capture the boy in his stronghold. Now that their vessel was cut to pieces, they had no means of leaving the island, and consequently they were prisoners there as well as Chase. He had this slight advantage of them, however: when the yacht arrived he would be set at liberty, while they would in all probability be secured and sent off to jail, where they belonged.

"I'll pay them for interfering with me when I wasn't troubling them," chuckled Chase, highly elated over the clever manner in which he had outwitted his captors. "I think I have managed affairs pretty well. Now, if the yacht would only come, I should be all right. It is to Walter's interest to assist me, if he only knew it; for I can tell him where Fred Craven is. But I can safely leave all that to Wilson. He is a friend worth having, and he will do all he can for me. What's going on out there, I wonder?"

The sound that had attracted the boy's attention was a scrambling among the bushes, accompanied by exclamations of anger and long-drawn whistles. The noise came down to him from the narrow crevice which extended to the top of the bluff, and from this Chase knew that Coulte and Pierre were ascending the rocks on the outside, and that they were having rather a difficult time of it. He wondered what they were going to do up there. They could not come down into the cave through the crevice, for it was so narrow that Fred Craven himself would have stuck fast in it. The boy took his stand under the opening and listened. He heard the two men toiling up the almost perpendicular sides, and knew when they reached the summit. Then there was a sound of piling wood, followed by the concussion of flint and steel; and presently a feeble flame, which gradually increased in volume, shot up from the top of the bluff.

"That's a signal," thought Chase, with some uneasiness. "Who in the world is abroad on the Gulf, on a night like this, that is likely to be attracted by it? It must be the smuggling vessel, for I remember hearing Mr. Bell say that he should start for Cuba this very night. I pity Fred Craven, shut up in that dark hold, with his hands and feet tied. I've had a little experience in that line to-night, and I know how it feels."

Chase seated himself on the floor of the cave, under the crevice, rested his head against the rocks, and set himself to watch the two men, whose movements he could distinctly see as they passed back and forth before the fire. In this position he went off into the land of dreams and slept for an hour, at the end of which time he awoke with a start, and a presentiment that some danger threatened him. He sprang to his feet, catching up his axe and looking all around the cave; and as he did so, a dark form, which had been stealthily creeping toward him, stopped and stretched itself out flat on the rocks, just in time to escape his notice.

"Was it a dream?" muttered Chase, rubbing his eyes. "I thought some one had placed a pole against the bluff and climbed into the cave; but of course that couldn't be, for Coulte and his son have no axe with which to cut a pole."

The boy once more glanced suspiciously about his hiding-place, which, from some cause, seemed to be a great deal lighter now than it was when he went to sleep, and hurrying to the mouth looked down into the gully below. To his consternation, he found that the danger he had apprehended in his dream was threatening him in reality. A pole had been placed against the ledge at the entrance to the cave, and clinging to it was the figure of a man, who had ascended almost to the top. It was Pierre. How he had managed to possess himself of the pole was a question Chase asked himself, but which he could not stop to answer. His enemy was too near and time too precious for that.

"Hold on!" shouted Pierre, when he saw the boy swing his axe aloft.

"You had better hold on to something solid yourself," replied Chase, "or you will go to the bottom of the ravine. You are as near to me as I care to have you come."

The axe descended, true to its aim, and cutting into the pole at the point where it touched the ledge severed it in twain, and sent Pierre heels-over-head to the ground. When this had been done, and Chase's excitement had abated so that he could look about him, he found that he had more than one enemy to contend with. He was astonished beyond measure at what he saw, and he knew now why "The Kitchen" was not as dark as it had been an hour before. The whole cove below him was brilliantly lighted up by a fire which had been kindled on the beach, and the most prominent object revealed to his gaze was a little schooner which was moored to the trees. The sight of her recalled most vividly to his mind the adventure of which he and Fred Craven had been the heroes. It was the Stella— the smuggling vessel. Her crew were gathered in a group at the bottom of the gully, and Chase's attention had been so fully occupied with Pierre that he had not seen them. As he ran his eye over the group he saw that there was one man in it besides Pierre who was anything but a stranger to him, and that was Mr. Bell, who stood a little apart from the others, with his tarpaulin drawn down over his forehead, and his arms buried to the elbows in the pockets of his pea-jacket. Remembering the uniform kindness and courtesy with which he and Wilson had been treated by that gentleman, while they were Bayard's guests and sojourners under his roof Chase was almost on the point of appealing to him for protection; but checked himself when he recalled the scene that had transpired on board the Stella, when he and Fred Craven were discovered in the hold.

"I'll not ask favors of a smuggler—an outlaw," thought Chase, tightening his grasp on his trusty axe. "It would be of no use, for it was through him that I was brought to this island."

"Look here, young gentleman," said a short, red-whiskered man, stepping out from among his companions, after holding a short consultation with Mr. Bell, "we want you."

"I can easily believe that," answered Chase. "I know too much to be allowed to remain at large, don't I? I don't want you. however."

"We've got business with you," continued the

red-whiskered man, who was the commander of the Stella, "and you had better listen to reason before we use force. Drop that axe and come down here."

"I think I see myself doing it. I'd look nice, surrendering myself into your hands, to be shut up in that dark hole with poor Fred Craven, carried to Cuba and shipped off to Mexico, under a Spanish sea-captain, wouldn't I? There's a good deal of reason in that, isn't there now? I'll fight as long as I can swing this axe."

"But that will do you no good," replied the captain, "for you are surrounded and can't escape. Where is Coulte?" he added, in an impatient undertone, to the men who stood about him.

"Surrounded!" thought Chase. He glanced quickly behind him, but could see nothing except the darkness that filled the cave, and that was something of which he was not afraid. "I'll have friends here before long," he added, aloud, "and until they arrive, I can hold you all at bay. I will knock down the poles as fast as you put them up."

"Where is Coulte, I wonder?" said the master of the smuggling vessel, again. "Why isn't he doing something? I could have captured him a dozen times."

These words reached the boy's ear, and the significant, earnest tone in which they were uttered, aroused his suspicions, and made him believe that perhaps the old Frenchman was up to something that might interest him. It might be that his enemies had discovered some secret passage-way leading into his stronghold, and had sent Coulte around to attack him in the rear. Alarmed at the thought, Chase no longer kept his back turned toward the cave, but stood in such a position that he could watch the farther end of "The Kitchen" and the men below at the same time.

A long silence followed the boy's bold avowal of his determination to stand his ground, during which time a whispered consultation was carried on by Mr. Bell, Pierre, and the captain of the schooner. When it was ended, the former led the way toward the beach, followed by all the vessel's company. Chase watched them until they disappeared among the bushes that lined the banks of the gully, and when they came out again and took their stand about the fire, he seated himself on the ledge at the entrance of the cave, and waited with no little uneasiness to see what they would do next.

"I know now what that fire on the bluff was for," thought he. "It was a signal to the smugglers, and they saw it and ran in here while I was asleep. They came very near capturing me, too—in a minute more Pierre would have been in the cave. I can't expect to fight a whole ship's company, and of course I must give in, sooner or later; but I will hold out as long as I can."

Chase finished his soliloquy with an exclamation, and jumped to his feet in great excitement. A thrill of hope shot through his breast when he saw the Banner come suddenly into view from behind the point, and dart into the cove; but it quickly gave away to a feeling of intense alarm. His long-expected reinforcements had arrived at last, but would they be able to render him the assistance he had hoped and longed for? Would they not rather bring themselves into serious trouble by running directly into the power of the smugglers? Forgetful of himself, and thinking only of the welfare of Walter and his companions, Chase dropped his axe and began shouting and waving his arms about his head to attract their attention.

3

"Get away from here!" he cried. "That vessel is the smuggler, and Fred Craven is a prisoner on board of her."

Walter heard the words of warning and so did all of his crew; but they came too late. The yacht was already beyond control. When her captain picked himself up from the deck where the shock of the collision had thrown him, and looked around to see where he was, he found the Banner's fore-rigging foul of the wreck of the schooner's bowsprit, and her stern almost high and dry, and jammed in among the bushes and trees on the bank. Escape from such a situation was simply impossible. He glanced at the cave where he had seen Chase but he had disappeared; then he looked at his crew, whose faces were white with alarm; and finally he turned his attention to the smugglers who were gathered about the fire. He could not discover anything in their personal appearance, or the expression of their faces, calculated to allay the fears which Chase's words had aroused in his mind. They were a hard-looking lot—just such men as one would expect to see engaged in such business.

"Now I'll tell you what's a fact," whispered Perk, as the crew of the Banner gathered about the captain on the quarterdeck; "did you hear what Chase said? We know where Featherweight is now, don't we?"

"Yes, and we shall probably see the inside of his prison in less than five minutes," observed Eugene. "Or else the smugglers will put us ashore and destroy our yacht, so that we can't leave the island until we are taken off."

"I don't see what in the world keeps the tug and the revenue-cutter," said Walter, anxiously. "They ought to have beaten us here, and unless they arrive very soon we shall be in serious trouble. What brought that schooner to the island, any how?"

"That is easily accounted for," returned Wilson, "Pierre is a member of the gang, as you are aware, and his friends probably knew that he was here, and stopped to take him off. Having brought their vessel into the cove, of course they must stay here until the wind goes down."

"Well, if they are going to do anything with us I wish they would be in a hurry about it," said Bab. "I don't like to be kept in suspense."

The young sailors once more directed their attention to the smugglers, and told one another that they did not act much like men who made it a point to secure everybody who knew anything of their secret. They did not seem to be surprised at the yacht's sudden appearance, but it was easy enough to see that they were angry at the rough manner in which she had treated their vessel. Her commander had shouted out several orders to Walter as the Banner came dashing into the cove, but as the young captain could not pay attention to both him and Chase at the same moment, the orders had not been heard. When the little vessel swung around into the bushes, the master of the schooner sprang upon the deck of his own craft, followed by his crew.

"That beats all the lubberly handling of a yacht I ever saw in my life, and I've seen a good deal of it," said the red-whiskered captain, angrily. "Do you want the whole Gulf to turn your vessel in?"

"You're a lubber yourself," retorted Walter, who, although he considered himself a prisoner in hands of the smugglers, was not the one to listen tamely to any imputation cast upon his seamanship. "I can handle a craft of this size as well as anybody."

"I don't see it," answered the master of the schooner. "My vessel is larger than yours, and I brought her in here without smashing everything in pieces."

"That may be. But the way was clear, and you came in under entirely different circumstances."

"Well, if you will bear a hand over there we will clear away this wreck. I want to go out again as soon as this wind goes down."

Wondering why the captain of the smugglers did not tell them that they were his prisoners, Walter and his crew went to work with the schooner's company, and by the aid of hatchets, handspikes, and a line made fast to a tree on the bank, succeeded in getting the little vessels apart; after which the Banner was hauled out into deep water and turned about in readiness to sail out of the cove. Walter took care, however, to work his vessel close in to the bank, in order to leave plenty of room for the tug and the revenue cutter when they came in. How closely he watched the entrance to the cove, and how impatiently he awaited their arrival!

While the crew of the schooner was engaged in repairing the wreck of the bowsprit, Walter and his men were setting things to rights on board the yacht, wondering exceedingly all the while. They did not understand the matter at all. Pierre and

Coulte had brought Chase to the island, intending to leave him to starve, freeze, or be taken off as fate or luck might decree, and all because he had learned something they did not want him to know. Fred Craven was a prisoner on board the very vessel that now lay alongside them, and that proved that he knew something about the smugglers also. Now, if the band had taken two boys captive because they had discovered their secret, and they did not think it safe to allow them to be at liberty, what was the reason they did not make an effort to secure the crew of the Banner? These were the points that Walter and his men were turning over in their minds, and the questions they propounded to one another, but not one of them could find an answer to them.

"Perhaps they think we might resist, and that we are too strong to be successfully attacked," said Eugene, at length.

"Hardly that, I imagine," laughed Walter. "Five boys would not be a mouthful for ten grown men."

"I say, fellows," exclaimed Bab, "what has become of Chase all of a sudden?"

"That's so!" cried all the crew in a breath, stopping their work and looking up at the bluffs above them. "Where is he?"

"The first and last I saw of him he was standing in the mouth of 'The Kitchen,'" continued Eab. "Where could he have gone, and why doesn't he come back and talk to us? Was he still a prisoner, or had he succeeded in escaping?"

"Well—I—declare, fellows," whispered Eugene, in great excitement, pointing to a gentleman dressed in broadcloth, who was lying beside the fire with his hat over his eyes, as if fast asleep, "if that isn't Mr. Bell I never saw him before."

The Banner's crew gazed long and earnestly at the prostrate man (if they had been a little nearer to him they would have seen that his eyes were wide open, and that he was closely watching every move they made from under the brim of his hat), and the whispered decision of each was that it was Mr. Bell. They knew him, in spite of his pea-jacket and tarpaulin. Was he a smuggler? He must be or else he would not have been there. He must be their leader, too, for a man like Mr. Bell would never occupy a subordinate position among those rough fellows. The young captain and his crew were utterly confounded by this new discovery. The mysteries surrounding them seemed to deepen every moment.

"What did I say, yesterday, when Walter finished reading that article in the paper?" asked Perk, after a long pause. "Didn't I tell you that if we had got into a fight with Bayard and his crowd, we would have whipped three of the relatives of the ringleader of the band?"

"Well, what's to be done?" asked Eugene. "We don't want to sit here inactive, while Chase is up in that cave, and Fred Craven a prisoner on board the schooner. One may be in need of help, the other certainly is, and we ought to bestir ourselves. Suggest something, somebody."

"Let us act as though we suspected nothing wrong, and go ashore and make some inquiries of Mr. Bell concerning Chase and the pirogue," said Walter. "We're here, we can't get away as long as this gale continues, and we might as well put a bold face on the matter."

"That's the idea. Shall somebody stay on board to keep an eye on the deserters?"

"I hardly think it will be necessary. They'll not be able to work their way out of the hold before we return."

"But the smugglers might take possession of the vessel."

"If that is their intention, our presence or absence will make no difference to them. They can take the yacht now as easily as they could if we were ashore."

Walter's suggestion being approved by the crew, they sprang over the rail, and walking around the cove—the Banner was moored at the bank opposite the fire—came up to the place where Mr. Bell was lying. He started up at the sound of their footsteps, and rubbing his eyes as if just aroused from a sound sleep, said pleasantly:

"You young gentlemen must be very fond of yachting, to venture out on a night like this. Did you come in here to get out of reach of the wind?"

"No, sir," replied Walter. "We expected to find Henry Chase on the island."

"And he is somewhere about here, too," exclaimed Wilson. "We saw him standing in the mouth of 'The Kitchen,' not fifteen minutes ago."

"The Kitchen!" echoed Mr. Bell, raising himself on his elbow and looking up at the cave in question. "Why, how could he get up there, and we know nothing about it? We've been here more than an hour."

"Haven't you seen him?" asked Walter.

"No."

"But you must have heard him shouting to us when we came into the cove."

"Why no, I did not," replied Mr. Bell, with an air of surprise. "In the first place, what object could he have in visiting the island, alone, on a night like this? And in the next, how could he come here without a boat?"

"There ought to be a boat somewhere about here," said Walter, while his companions looked wonderingly at one another, "because Pierre and Coulte brought him over here in a pirogue."

It now seemed Mr. Bell's turn to be astonished. He looked hard at Walter, as if trying to make up his mind whether or not he was really in earnest, and then a sneering smile settled on his face; and stretching himself out on his blanket again he pulled his hat over his eyes, remarking as he did so:

"All I have to say is, that Chase was a blockhead to let them do it."

"Now just listen to me a minute, Mr. Bell, and

I'll tell you what's a fact," said Perk, earnestly. "He couldn't help it, for he was tied hard and fast."

The gentleman lifted his hat from his eyes, gazed at Perk a moment, smiled again, and said: "Humph!"

"I know it is so," insisted Perk, "because I saw him and had hold of him. I had hold of Coulte too; and if I get my hands on him again to-night, he won't escape so easily."

"What object could the old Frenchman and his son have had in tying Chase hand and foot, and taking him to sea in a dugout?"

"Their object was to get him out of the way," said Walter. "Chase knows that Coulte's two sons belong to a gang of smugglers, and they wanted to put him where he would have no opportunity to communicate his discovery to anybody."

"Smugglers!" repeated the gentleman, in a tone of voice that was exceedingly aggravating. "Smugglers about Bellville? Humph."

"Yes sir, smugglers," answered Wilson, with a good deal of spirit. "And we have evidence that you will perhaps put some faith in—the word of your own son."

"O, I am not disputing you, young gentlemen," said Mr. Bell, settling his hands under his head, and crossing his feet as if he were preparing to go to sleep. "I simply say that your story looks to me rather unreasonable; and I would not advise you to repeat it in the village for fear of getting yourselves into trouble. I have not seen Pierre, or Coulte, or Chase to-night. Perhaps the captain has, or some of his men, although it is hardly probable. As I am somewhat wearied with my day's work, I hope you will allow me to go to sleep."

"Certainly, sir," said Walter. "Pardon us for disturbing you."

So saying, the young commander of the Banner turned on his heel and walked off, followed by his crew.

CHAPTER III.

OUTWITTED.

"WELL," continued Walter, after he and his companions had walked out of earshot of Mr. Bell; "what do you think of that."

"Let somebody else tell," said Bab. "It bangs me completely."

"Now I'll tell you something," observed Perk: "He is trying to humbug us—I could see it in his eye. If there is a fellow among us who didn't see Henry Chase standing in the mouth of the cave, when we rounded the point, and hear him shout to us that that schooner there is a smuggler, and that Fred Craven is a prisoner on board of her, let him say so."

Perk paused, and the Banner's crew looked at one another, but no one spoke. They had all seen Chase, and had heard and understood his words.

"That is proof enough that Chase is on the

island," said Walter, "for it is impossible that five of us should have been so deceived. Now, if *we* heard and saw him, what's the reason Mr. Bell didn't? That pirogue must be hidden about here somewhere. If you fellows will look around for it, I will go back to the yacht, see how our deserters are getting on, and bring a lantern and an axe. Then we'll go up and give 'The Kitchen' a thorough overhauling."

Walter hurried off, and his crew began beating about through the bushes, looking for the pirogue. They searched every inch of the ground they passed over, peeping into hollow logs, and up into the branches of the trees, and examining places in which one of the paddles of the canoe could scarcely have been stowed away, but without success. There was one place however, where they did not look, and that was *in the fire*, beside which Mr. Bell lay. Had they thought of that, they might have found something.

When Walter returned with the axe and the lighted lantern, the crew reported the result of their search, and the young captain, disappointed and more perplexed than ever, led the way toward "The Kitchen." While they were going up the gully, they stopped to cut a pole, with which to ascend to the cave, and looked everywhere for signs of anybody having passed along the path that night; but it was dark among the bushes, and the light of the lantern revealed not a single foot-print. Arriving at the bluff, they placed the pole against the ledge, and climbing up one after the other, entered the cave, leaving Eugene at the mouth to keep an eye on the yacht, and on the movements of the smugglers below. But their search here was also fruitless. There was the wood which the last visitors from the village had provided to cook their meals, the dried leaves that had served them for a bed, and the remains of their camp-fire; but that was all. The axe that had done Chase such good service, his blankets, bacon, and everything else he had brought there, as well as the boy himself, had disappeared.

Eugene, who was deeply interested in the movements of his companions, did not perform the part of watchman very well. On two or three occasions he left his post and entered the cave to assist in the search; and once when he did this, Mr. Bell, who still kept his recumbent position by the fire, made a sign with his hand, whereupon two men glided from the bushes that lined the beach, and clambering quickly over the side of the smuggling vessel, crept across the deck and dived into the hold. Eugene returned to the mouth of the cave just as they went down the ladder, but did not see them.

"Now then," said Walter, when the cave had been thoroughly searched, "some of you fellows who are good at unravelling mysteries, explain this. What has become of Chase? Did he leave the cave of his own free will, and if so, how did he get out? We found no pole by which he could have descended, and consequently he must have hung by his hands from the ledge and dropped to the ground. But he would not have done that for fear of a sprained ankle. He surely did not allow any one to come up here and take him out, for with a handful of these rocks he could have held the cave against a dozen men. Besides, he would have shouted for help, and we should have heard him."

None of the crew had a word to say in regard to Chase's mysterious disappearance. They sighed deeply, shook their heads, and looked down at the ground, thus indicating quite as plainly as they could have done by words, that the matter was altogether too deep for their comprehension. More bewildered than ever, they followed one another down the pole, and retraced their steps toward the beach.

"What shall we do to pass away the time until the tug and cutter arrive?" asked Perk. "I wish that schooner could find a tongue long enough to tell us what she's got stowed away in her hold."

"If she could, and told you the truth, she would assure you that Fred Craven is there," said Wilson, confidently. "Of that I am satisfied. He's on some vessel, for Chase told me so while we were at Coulte's cabin. If this schooner is an honest merchantman, why did she come in here? There's nothing the matter with her that I can see. She didn't come in to get out of the wind, for she can certainly stand any sea that the Banner can outride. Coulte and his sons belong to the smugglers, because I heard Bayard say so. Chase told me that he was to be carried to the island in a pirogue, and we met her as she came down the bayou. Now, put these few things together, and to my mind they explain the character of this vessel and the reason why she is here."

"Go on," said Eugene. "Put a few other things together, and see if you can explain where Chase went in such a hurry."

4

"That is beyond me quite. But the matter will be cleared up in a very few minutes," added Wilson, gleefully, "for here comes the cutter."

As he spoke, the revenue vessel came swiftly around the point; and so overjoyed were the boys to see her, that they swung their hats around their heads and greeted her with cheers that awoke a thousand echoes among the bluffs. Being better handled than the Banner was when she came in, she glided between the two vessels lying in the cove, and running her bowsprit among the bushes on the bank, came to a stand still without even a jar. Her captain had evidently made preparations to perform any work he might find to do without the loss of a moment; for no sooner had the cutter swung round broadside to the bank, than a company of men with small-arms tumbled over the side, followed by the second lieutenant, and finally by the commander himself.

"Here we are again, captain," said the latter, as Walter came up, "and all ready for business. Bring on your smugglers."

"There they are, sir," answered Walter, pointing to the crew of the schooner, who had once more congregated about the fire, "and there's their vessel."

"That!" exclaimed the second lieutenant, opening his eyes in surprise. "You're mistaken, captain. That is the Stella—a trader from Bellville, bound for Havana, with an assorted cargo—hams, bacon, flour, and the like. I boarded her to-night and examined her papers myself. She no doubt put in here on account of stress of weather."

"Stress of weather!" repeated Walter, contemptuously. "That little yacht has come from Bellville since midnight, and never shipped a bucket of water; and the schooner is four times as large as she is. Stress of weather, indeed!"

"Well, she is all right, any how."

"I am sure, captain, that if you will take the trouble to look into things a little, you will find that she is *not* all right—begging the lieutenant's pardon for differing with him so decidedly," said Walter. "Some strange things have happened since we came here."

"Well, captain, I will satisfy you on that point, seeing that you are so positive," replied the commander of the revenue vessel. "Mr. Harper," he added, turning to the lieutenant, "send your men on board the cutter and come with me."

A landsman would have seen no significance in this order, but Walter and his crew did, and they were not at all pleased to hear it. The sending of the men back on board the vessel was good evidence that the revenue captain did not believe a word they said, and that he was going to "look into things," merely to satisfy what he thought to be a boyish curiosity. It is not likely that he would have done even this much, had he not been aware that the young sailors had influential friends on shore who might have him called to account for any neglect of duty. Walter's disgust and indignation increased as they approached the fire. The men composing the crew of the smuggling vessel stepped aside to allow them to pass, and Mr. Bell advanced with outstretched hand, to greet the revenue captain.

"Why, how is this?" exclaimed the latter, accepting the proffered hand and shaking it heartily. "I did not expect to find you here, Mr. Bell. Ah! Captain Conway, good morning to you," he added, addressing the red-whiskered master of the schooner. "Captain Gaylord, there is no necessity of carrying this thing any farther. The presence of these two gentlemen, with both of whom I am well acquainted, is as good evidence as I want that the schooner is not a smuggler."

"A smuggler!" repeated the master of the Stella.

"Why, what is the matter?" asked Mr. Bell, opening his eyes in surprise, and looking first at Walter, and then at the revenue captain, while the crew of the schooner crowded up to hear what was going on.

"Why the truth is, that this young gentleman has got some queer ideas into his head concerning your vessel. He thinks she is the smuggler of which I have been so long in search."

"And I have the best of reasons for thinking so," said Walter; not in the least terrified or abashed by the angry glances that were directed toward him from all sides. "In the first place, does she not correspond with the description you have in your possession?"

"I confess that she does," replied the revenue captain, running his eye over the schooner from cross-trees to water-line.

"She answers the description much better than the yacht, does she not?"

"Yes. But then she has papers, which my lieutenant has examined, and I know these two gentlemen. You had no papers, and I was not acquainted with a single man on board your vessel."

"A smuggler!" repeated the red-whiskered captain, angrily; "I don't believe there's such a thing in the Gulf."

"I am inclined to agree with you," answered the revenue commander. "I have looked everywhere, without finding one."

"I own the cargo with which this vessel is loaded," said Mr. Bell, producing his pocket-book, and handing some papers to the revenue captain, who returned them without looking at them, "and there are the receipts of the merchants from whom I purchased it. I am a passenger on her because I believe that, by going to Cuba, I can dispose of the cargo to much better advantage than I could sell it through agents. That is why I am here."

"And the schooner is heavily loaded, and I couldn't make the run without straining her," said the master of the Stella. "Having got into the cove I must wait until the wind dies away before I can go out. That's why *I* am here."

The commander of the cutter listened with an air which said very plainly, that this was all unnecessary

—that he had made up his mind and it could not be changed—and then turned to Walter as if to ask what he had to say in reply.

"What these men have said may be true and it may not," declared the young captain, boldly. "The way to ascertain is to search the schooner. There are some articles on board of her that are not down in her bills of lading."

"And if there are it is no business of mine," returned the commander of the cutter.

"It isn't!" exclaimed Walter in great amazement. "Then I'd like to know just how far a revenue officer's business extends. Haven't you authority to search any vessel you suspect?"

"Certainly I have; but I don't suspect this schooner. And, even if I did, I would not search her now, because she is outward bound. If she has contraband articles on board, the Cuban revenue officers may look to it, for I will not. All I have to do is to prevent, as far as lies in my power, articles from being smuggled *into* the United States; I don't care a snap what goes *out*."

"But you ought to care. There is a boy on board that schooner, held as a prisoner."

"Why is he held as a prisoner?"

"Because he knows something about the smugglers, and they are afraid to allow him his liberty.'

"Humph!" exclaimed Mr. Bell.

"Every word of that is false," cried the master of the Stella, who seemed to be almost beside himself with fury. "It is a villainous attempt to injure me and my vessel."

"Keep your temper, captain," said the commander of the cutter. "I want to see if this young man knows what he is talking about. Where are those two smugglers who brought that boy over here in a canoe?"

"I don't know, sir. We have searched the island and can find no trace of them."

"That is a pretty good sign that they are not here. Where is the boat they came in?"

"I don't know that either. It is also missing."

"Where is the boy they brought with them?"

"When the Banner rounded the point he was standing in the mouth of that cave," replied Walter, pointing to the Kitchen, "and shouted to us to get away from here while we could—that this schooner is a smuggler and that Fred Craven is a prisoner on board of her."

"Well, where is the boy now?"

"I can't tell you, sir."

"Isn't he on the island?"

"We can find no signs of him."

"Then he hasn't been here to-night."

"He certainly has," replied Walter, "for we saw him and heard him too."

"Who did?"

"Every one of the crew of the Banner."

"Did anybody else? Did you, Mr. Bell? Or you, Captain Conway? Or any of your men?"

The persons appealed to answered with a most decided negative. They had seen no boy in the cave, heard no voice, and knew nothing about a prisoner or a pirogue. There was one thing they did know, however, and that was that no dugout that was ever built could traverse forty miles of the Gulf in such a sea as that which was running last night.

"Well, young man," said the revenue officer, addressing the captain of the yacht somewhat sternly, "I am sure I don't know what to think of you."

"You are at liberty to think what you please, sir," replied Walter, with spirit. "I have told you the truth, if you don't believe it search that schooner."

"You have failed to give me any reason why I should do so. Your story is perfectly ridiculous. You say that a couple of desperate smugglers captured an acquaintance of yours and put him in a canoe; that you met them in a bayou on the main shore and had a fight with them; that they eluded you and came out into the Gulf in a gale that no small boat in the world could stand, and brought their prisoner to this island. When I expressed a reasonable doubt of the story, you offered, if I would come here with you, to substantiate every word of it. Now I am here, and you can not produce a scrap of evidence to prove that you are not trying to make game of me. The men, the boy, and the boat they came in, are not to be found. I wouldn't advise you to repeat a trick of this kind or you may learn to your cost that it is a serious matter to trifle with a United States officer when in the discharge of his duty. Mr. Bell, as the wind has now subsided so that I can go out, I wish you good-by and a pleasant voyage,"

"One moment, captain," said Walter, as the revenue commander was about to move off; "perhaps you will think I am trifling with you, if I tell you that I have some deserters from your vessel on board my yacht."

"Have you? I am glad to hear it. I have missed them, and I know who they are. I thought they had gone ashore at Bellville, and it was by stopping to look for them that I lost so much time. Haul your yacht alongside the cutter and put them aboard."

"I am going to set them at liberty right where the yacht lies," replied Walter, indignant at the manner in which the revenue captain had treated him, and at the insolent tone of voice in which the order was issued; "and you can stand by to take charge of them or not, just as you please."

"How many of them are there?"

"Two."

"Only two? Then the others must have gone ashore at Bellville, after all," added the captain, turning to his second lieutenant. "I wish they had taken your vesssel out of your hands and run away with it. You need bringing down a peg or two, worse than any boy I ever saw."

Walter, without stopping to reply, turned on his heel, and walked around the cove to the place where the Banner lay, followed by his crew, who gave vent to their astonishment and indignation in no measured terms. The deserters were released at once. When informed that their vessel was close at hand, and that their captain was expecting them, they ascended to the deck, looking very much disappointed and crestfallen, and stood in the waist until the cutter came alongside and took them off. They were both powerful men, and the boy-tars were glad indeed that they had been discovered before they gained a footing on deck. If Walter had been in his right mind he would have examined the hold after those two men left it; but he was so bewildered by the strange events that had transpired since he came into the cove, that he could think of nothing else.

While the crew of the yacht were liberating the deserters, the smuggling vessel filled away for the Gulf—her captain springing upon the rail long enough to shake his fist at Walter—and as soon as she was fairly out of the cove, the cutter followed, and shaped her course toward Bellville.

The boys watched the movements of the two vessels in silence, and when they had passed behind the point out of sight, turned with one accord to

Walter, who was thoughtfully pacing his quarter-deck, with his hands behind his back.

"Eugene," said the young captain, at length, "did you keep an eye on the smuggler all the time that we were in The Kitchen."

"O, yes," replied Eugene, confidently. "I saw everything that happened on her deck." And he thought he did, but he forgot that he had two or three times left his post.

"You didn't see Chase taken on board the schooner, did you?"

"I certainly did not. If I had, I should have said something about it."

"Then there is only one explanation to this mystery: Chase was somehow spirited out of the cave and hidden on the island. We will make one more attempt to find him. Three of us will go ashore and thoroughly search these woods and cliffs, and the others stay and watch the yacht."

Walter, Perk, and Bab, after arming themselves with handspikes, sprang ashore and bent their steps toward The Kitchen to begin their search for the missing Chase. As before, no signs of him were found in the cave, although every nook and crevice large enough to conceal a squirrel, was peeped into.

Next the gully received a thorough examination, and finally they came to the bushes on the side of the bluff. A suspicious-looking pile of leaves under a rock attracted **Bab's** attention, and he thrust his handspike into it. The weapon came in contact with something which struggled feebly, and uttered a smothered, groaning sound, which made Bab start back in astonishment.

"What have you there?" asked Walter, from the foot of the bluff.

"I don't know, unless it is a varmint of some kind that has taken up his winter quarters here. Come up, and let's punch him out."

Perk and Walter clambered up the bluff to the ledge, and while one raised his handspike in readiness to deal the "varmint" a death-blow the instant he showed himself, the others cautiously pushed aside the leaves, and presently disclosed to view— not a wild animal, but a pair of heavy boots, the heels of which were armed with small silver spurs. One look at them was enough. With a common impulse the three boys dropped their handspikes, and pulling away the leaves with frantic haste, soon dragged into sight the missing boy, securely bound and gagged, and nearly suffocated. To give him the free use of his hands and feet, and remove the stick that was tied between his teeth, was but the work of a moment. When this had been done, Chase slowly raised himself to a sitting posture, gasping for breath, and looking altogether pretty well used up.

"You don't know how grateful I am to you, fellows," said he, at last, speaking in a hoarse whisper. "I've had a hard time of it during the half hour I have been stowed away in that hole, and I never expected to see daylight again."

"Now I'll tell you what's a fact," said Perk. "You never would have got out of there alive if Walter hadn't been thoughtful enough to search the island before going home. Now let me ask you something: Where did you go in such a hurry, after shouting to us from the mouth of The Kitchen?"

"I can't talk much, fellows, till I get something to moisten my tongue," was the almost indistinct reply. "If you will help me to the spring, I will tell you all about it. Where are the smugglers?"

"Don't know. We haven't seen any," said Walter.

"You haven't?" whispered Chase, in great

amazement. "Didn't you see those men who were standing on the beach when you came in?"

"Yes; but they are not smugglers. They've got clearance papers, and the captain of the cutter says he knows they are all right. Besides, one of of them was Mr. Bell."

"No difference; I know they are smugglers by their own confession, and that Mr. Bell is the leader of them. O, it's a fact, fellows; I know what I am talking about. Where are they now?"

"Gone."

"*Gone!* Where?"

"To Havana, most likely. That's the port their vessel cleared for."

"And did you rescue Fred Craven? I know you didn't by your looks. Well, you'll have to find that schooner again if you want to see him, for he's on board of her, and—wait till I rest awhile, fellows, and get a drink of water."

Seeing that it was with the greatest difficulty that Chase could speak, Perk and Walter lifted him to his feet, and assisted him to walk down the gully, while Bab followed after, carrying the handspikes on his shoulder. Arriving at the spring, Chase lay down beside it and took a large and hearty drink, now and then pausing to testify to the satisfaction he felt by shaking his head, and uttering long-drawn sighs. After quenching his thirst, and taking a few turns up and down the path to stretch his arms and legs, he felt better.

CHAPTER IV.

FAIRLY AFLOAT.

"THE first thing, fellows," said Chase, "is to tell you that I am heartily sorry I have treated you so shabbily."

"Now, please don't say a word about that," interrupted Walter, kindly. "We don't think hard of you for anything you have done, and besides we have more important matters to talk about."

"I know how ready you are, Walter Gaylord, to overlook an injury that is done you—you and the rest of the Club—and that is just what makes me feel so mean," continued Chase, earnestly. "I was not ashamed to wrong you, and I ought not to be ashamed to ask your forgiveness. I made up my mind yesterday, while we were disputing about those panther scalps (to which we had not the smallest shadow of a right, as we knew very well), to give Fred Craven a good thumping, if I was man enough to do it, for beating me in the race for Vice-

Commodore; and the next time I met him he paid me for it in a way I did not expect. He tried to assist me, and got himself into a terrible scrape by it."

"That is just what we want to hear about," said Bab, "and you are the only one who can enlighten us. But Eugene and Wilson would like to listen to the story also; and if you can walk so far, I suggest that we go on board the yacht."

"What do you suppose has become of Coulte and Pierre?" asked Walter. "Are they still on the island?"

"No, indeed," replied Chase. "If the rest of the smugglers are gone, of course they went with them."

After Chase had taken another drink from the spring, he accompanied his deliverers down the gully. The watch on board the yacht discovered them as they came upon the beach, and pulling off their hats, greeted them with three hearty cheers. When they reached the vessel, Wilson testified to the joy he felt at meeting his long-lost friend once more, by seizing him by the arms and dragging him bodily over the rail.

"One moment, fellows!" exclaimed Walter, and

his voice arrested the talking and confusion at once. "Chase, are you positive that Featherweight is a prisoner on board that schooner?"

"I am; and I know he will stay there until he reaches Havana, unless something turns up in his favor."

"Then we've not an instant to waste in talking," said the young captain. "We must keep that schooner in sight, if it is within the bounds of possibility. Get under way, Perk."

"Hurrah!" shouted Eugene, forgetting in the excitement of the moment the object for which their cruise was about to be undertaken. "Here's for a sail clear to Cuba."

"Now, just listen to me a minute and I'll tell you what's a fact," said Perk. "One reason why I fought so hard against those deserters was, because I was afraid that if they got control of the vessel they would take us out to sea; and now we are going out of our own free will."

"And with not a man on board;" chimed in Bab, "nobody to depend upon but ourselves. This will be something to talk about when we get back to Bellville, won't it?"

The crew worked with a will, and in a very few

minutes the Banner was once more breasting the waves of the Gulf, her prow being turned toward the West Indies. As soon as she was fairly out of the cove, a half a dozen pairs of eyes were anxiously directed toward the southern horizon, and there, about three miles distant, was the Stella, scudding along under all the canvas she could carry. The gaze of the young sailors was then directed toward the Louisiana shore; but in that direction not a craft of any kind was in sight, except the revenue cutter, and she was leaving them behind every moment. Exclamations of wonder arose on all sides, and every boy turned to Walter, as if he could tell them all about it, and wanted to know what was the reason the tug had not arrived.

"I don't understood it any better than you do, fellows," was the reply. "She ought to have reached the island in advance of us. And I don't see why the Lookout hasn't put in an appearance. If father and Uncle Dick reached home last night, they've had plenty of time to come to our assistance. It would do me good to see her come up and overhaul that schooner."

"Isn't that a cutter, off there?" asked Chase, who had been attentively regarding the revenue vessel through Walter's glass. "Let's signal to her She'll help us."

"Humph! See wouldn't pay the least attention to us; we've tried her. The captain wouldn't believe a word we said to him."

It was now about nine o'clock in the morning, and a cold, dismal morning it was, too. The gale of the night before had subsided into a capital sailing wind, but there was considerable sea running, and a suspicious-looking bank of clouds off to windward, which attracted the attention of the yacht's company the moment they rounded the point. The crew looked at Walter, and he looked first at the sky and clouds and then at the schooner. He had been on the Gulf often enough to know that it would not be many hours before the sea-going qualities of his little vessel, the nerve of her crew, and the skill on which he prided himself, would be put to a severer test than they had yet experienced, and for a moment he hesitated. But it was only for a moment. The remembrance of the events that had just transpired in the cove, the dangers with which Fred Craven was surrounded, and the determination he had more than once expressed to stand by him until he was rescued—all these things came into his mind, and his course was quickly decided upon. Although he said nothing, his crew knew what he was thinking about, and they saw by the expression which settled on his face that there was to be no backing out, no matter what happened.

"I was *dreadfully* afraid you were going to turn back, Walter," said Eugene, drawing a long breath of relief.

"I would have opposed such a proceeding as long as I had breath to speak or could think of a word to utter," said Perk. "Featherweight's salvation depends upon us entirely, now that the tug has failed to arrive and the cutter has gone back on us."

"But, fellows, we are about to undertake a bigger job than some of you have bargained for, perhaps," said Bab. "Leaving the storm out of the question, there is the matter of provisions. We have eaten nothing since yesterday at breakfast, and the lunch we brought on board last night will not make more than one hearty meal for six of us. We shall all have good appetites by the time we reach Havana, I tell you."

"I can see a way out of that difficulty," replied Walter. "We will soon be in the track of vessels bound to and from the Balize, and if we fall in with one of those little New Orleans traders, we will speak her and purchase what we want. I don't suppose any of us are overburdened with cash—I am not—but if we can raise ten or fifteen dollars, a trader will stop for that."

"I will pass around the hat and see how much we can scrape together," said Eugene, "and while I am doing that, suppose we listen to what Chase has to say for himself."

The young sailors moved nearer to the boy at the wheel so that he might have the benefit of the story, and while they were counting out their small stock of change and placing it in Eugene's hands, Chase began the account of his adventures. He went back to the time of the quarrel which Bayard Bell and his cousins had raised with himself and Wilson, told of the plan he and his companion had decided upon to warn Walter of his danger, and described how it was defeated by the smugglers. This much the Club had already heard from Wilson; but now Chase came to something of which they had not heard, and that was the incidents that transpired on the smuggling vessel. Walter and his companions listened in genuine amazement as Chase went on to describe the interview he had held with Bayard and

The Club Afloat.

his cousins (he laughed heartily at the surprise and indignation they had exhibited when they found him in the locker instead of Walter, although he had thought it anything but a laughing matter at the time), and to relate what happened after Fred Craven arrived. At this stage of his story Chase was often interrupted by exclamations of anger; and especially were the crew vehement in their expressions of wrath, when they learned that Featherweight's trials would by no means be ended when he reached Havana—that he was to be shipped as a foremast hand on board a Spanish vessel and sent off to Mexico. This was all that was needed to arouse the fiercest indignation against Mr. Bell. The thought that a boy like Fred Craven was to be forced into a forecastle, to be tyrannized over by some brute of a mate, ordered about in language that he could not understand, and perhaps knocked down with a belaying-pin or beaten with a rope's end, because he did not know what was required of him—this was too much; and Eugene in his excitement declared that if Walter would crack on and lay the yacht alongside the schooner, they would board her, engage in a hand-to-hand fight with the smugglers, and rescue the secretary at all hazards.

Had the young captain put this reckless proposition to a vote it would have been carried without a dissenting voice.

When the confusion had somewhat abated Chase went on with his story, and finally came to another event of which the Club had heard the particulars—the siege in Coulte's house. He described the sail down the bayou, the attempted rescue by the Club, the voyage to the island during the gale, the destruction of the pirogue, and his escape and retreat to The Kitchen. His listeners became more attentive than ever when he reached this point, and his mysterious manner increased their impatience to hear how he could have been spirited out of the cave without being seen by any one.

"It was a surprise to me," said Chase, "but it was done as easily as falling off a log. After I fell asleep the Stella, seeing the signal which Pierre and Coulte had lighted on the top of the bluff, came into the cove. I awoke just in time to keep Pierre from stealing a march upon me, but too late to prevent the entrance of Coulte. The old fellow must have come in just before I opened my eyes, and he was in the cave close behind me all the time I was talking to the smugglers; but he kept himself out of sight, thinking, no doubt, that it would not be a safe piece of business to attack me as long as I held my axe in my hand. The captain of the Stella told me that I was surrounded, and on two different occasions asked in a tone of voice loud enough for me to hear: 'Where is Coulte, and why don't he bestir himself?' This made me believe that there was something amiss, and I stood in such a position that I could keep an eye on the interior of the cave and watch the men below at the same time, thus giving Coulte no opportunity to take me at disadvantage. But when I saw the Banner come in, I forgot everything in the fear that if you did not immediately turn about and leave the cove, you would all be captured. Intent upon warning you I threw down my axe and shouted to attract your attention. This was just what the old Frenchman was waiting for. No sooner had the words I shouted out to you left my lips, than he jumped up and seized me; and before I could say 'hard a starboard' I was helpless, being bound and gagged. I had no idea the old fellow possessed so much muscle and activity. He handled me as if I had been an infant."

"But how did he ever get you down from the cave without being seen by some of us?" asked Eugene.

"O, he had opportunities enough," said Bab—"while we were getting our vessel free from the schooner and out of the bushes for instance."

"Or while we were talking with Mr. Bell," said Wilson.

"He might have done it while we were looking for the pirogue, or at any time within ten minutes after we entered the cove," remarked Walter. "I for one was so much astonished at what I saw and heard when we came around the point, that, after Chase ceased speaking to us, I never thought of him again until we had got our vessel moored to the bank."

"I can't tell *when* it was done, fellows," continued Chase, "but I know it *was* done. As soon as Coulte had secured me, he looked out of the cave, waved his hand once or twice, and then began throwing out the articles he had given me for an outfit. Perhaps he thought you might look in 'The Kitchen' for me before you left the island, and he didn't think it best to leave any traces of me there. In a few minutes Pierre came up with a rope over his shoulders. This they made fast under my arms, and watching their opportunity, when your attention was engaged with something else, they lowered me into the gully. They then followed me down the pole by which Pierre had come up, and hid me away under the rocks where you found me."

And Chase might have added that after they had disposed of him, they went on board the smuggling vessel and concealed themselves in the hold until she was safe out of the cove. But this was something of which he had no positive evidence. In a few days, however, the crew met some one who told them all about it, and then Eugene, to his great surprise, learned that if he had faithfully performed the part Walter had assigned him, he might have been able to make a great change in the fortunes of Fred Craven. He could then have revealed to the revenue captain the whereabouts of the men who had captured Chase and brought him to the island, and that gentleman might have been induced to look into the matter.

When Chase finished his story, and the Club had questioned him to their satisfaction, he expressed a desire to hear what had happened to them since they last met. Eugene spoke for his companions, and it is certain that there was not another member of the Club who could have described their adventures in more glowing language, or shown up the obstinacy and stupidity of the revenue captain, in a more damaging light. Eugene said he could not tell what had become of the remains of the pirogue, or tell how Coulte and Pierre had left the island; but he made everything else clear to Chase, who, when the story was finished, was as indignant as any of the Club. The incidents of the interview with Mr. Bell were thoroughly discussed, and the conclusion arrived at was, that they had been very nicely outwitted; that the smugglers had played their part to perfection; and that the revenue captain was totally unfit for the position he held.

During the next hour nothing worthy of record transpired on board the yacht. Walter kept as much sail on her as she could carry, and although she did splendidly, as the heaving of the log proved, she moved much too slowly to suit her impatient crew. Directly in advance, apparently no nearer and no farther away than when the pursuit began, was the smuggling vessel; and in the west was that angry-looking cloud, whose approach the boy-sailors awaited with no little uneasiness.

Having had their talk out, Fred Craven's mysterious disappearance having been fully explained, and knowing that nothing could be done to assist him until the schooner was overtaken and help obtained from some source, the crew of the Banner began to busy themselves about matters that demanded their immediate attention, with a view to making their voyage across the Gulf as safe and agreeable as possible. The first thing to be done was to put Chase and Wilson at their ease. Now that their excitement had somewhat worn away, these young gentlemen began to look upon themselves as interlopers, and to wish that they were anywhere but on board the yacht. Their desire to assist Featherweight was as strong as ever, but remembering all that had passed, and judging the Club by themselves, they believed that their absence would have suited Walter and his friends quite as well as their company. Nothing had been done, a word said, or a look given to make them think so, but the manner in which they conducted themselves showed plainly enough that such was their impression. They took no part in the conversation now, answered the questions that were asked them only in monosyllables, and exhibited a desire to get away from the crew and keep by themselves. The Club saw and understood it all, and tried hard to make them believe that all old differences had been for gotten, and that their offers of friendship were sincere. When lunch was served up—the last crumb the baskets contained was eaten, for Walter said that one square meal would do them more good than two or three scanty ones—the Club made them talk by asking them all sorts of questions, and requesting their advice as to their future operations; and Eugene even went so far as to offer Wilson the bow-oar of the Spray to pull in the next regatta—a position which he regarded as a post of honor, and which, under ordinary circumstances, he would have been loth to surrender to his best friend. Wilson declined, but Eugene insisted, little dreaming that when the next regatta came off, the Spray would be locked up in the boat-house and covered with dust, while he and the rest of her gallant crew would be thousands of miles away.

By the time lunch had been disposed of, the Club, by their united efforts, had succeeded in dispelling all doubts from the minds of their late enemies, and harmony and good feeling began to prevail. While the dishes were being packed away in the baskets, Wilson discovered a sail which he pointed out to Walter, who, with his glass in his hand, ascended to the cross-trees. After a few minutes' examination of the stranger, he came down again, and the course of the Banner was altered so as to intercept the approaching vessel. At the end of an hour she was in plain sight, and proved to be a schooner about the size of the Stella—a coaster, probably. In thirty minutes more the two vessels were hove-to within speaking distance of each other; Walter, with his trumpet in his hand was perched upon the yacht's rail, and the master of the schooner stood with one hand grasping the shrouds and the other behind his ear, waiting to hear what was said to him.

"Schooner ahoy!" shouted Walter.

"Ay! ay! sir!" was the answer.

"I have no provisions; can you spare me some?"

The captain of the schooner, after gazing up at the clouds and down at the water, asked: "How much do you want?"

"How much money did you raise, Eugene?" asked the young commander, turning to his brother.

"Thirty dollars. And that's every cent there is on board the yacht."

"About twenty-five dollars worth," shouted Walter.

"What sort?"

"Every sort—beef, pork, coffee, sugar, biscuit, and some fresh vegetables, if you have them. I haven't a mouthful on board."

After a short time spent in conversation with a man who stood at his side, during which he was doubtless expressing his astonishment that the commander of any craft should be foolish enough to venture so far from land without a mouthful of provisions for himself and crew, the captain of the schooner called out:

"All right. I reckon I shall have to take them aboard of you?'

"Yes, sir. I have no small boat to send after them."

The captain walked away from the rail, and the young yachtsmen, overjoyed at their success, began to express their appreciation of his kindness in no measured terms. It wasn't every shipmaster who would have sold them the provisions, and not one in a hundred who would have sent his own boat to bring them aboard.

"It is the money he is after," said Walter. "These little traders will do almost anything to turn a penny. Now Chase, hold her just as she is, as nearly as you can. Eugene, open the fore-hatch and rig a block and tackle; and the rest of us turn to and get up some boxes and barrels from the hold to stow the provisions in."

The crew, headed by Walter carrying a lighted lantern, went down into the galley and opened the hold. What was the reason they did not hear the strange sounds that came up from below as they threw back the hatch? They might have heard them if they had not been so busy thinking and talking about something else—sounds that would have created a panic among them at once, for they strongly resembled the shuffling of feet and angry excited whispering. It was dark in the hold in spite of the light the lantern threw out, or Walter, as he leaped through the hatchway, might have seen the figure which crept swiftly away and hid itself behind one of the water-butts.

The barrels for the pork, beef, fresh vegetables and biscuit, and the boxes for the coffee and sugar were quickly selected by Walter and passed up to Wilson in the galley, who in turn handed them up to Bab through the fore-hatchway. When this had been done the boys below returned to the deck and waited for the schooner's yawl, which soon made its appearance, rowed by four sailors and steered by the captain.

Judging by the size of the load in the boat they had a liberal man to deal with, for he was bringing them a goodly supply of provisions in return for their promised twenty-five dollars. When he came alongside the yacht he sprang over the rail and gazed about him with a good deal of surprise and curiosity.

"Where's the captain?" he asked.

"Here I am, sir," replied Walter.

The master of the schooner stared hard at the boy, then at each of his companions, ran his eye over the deck and rigging of the little vessel, which was doubtless cleaner and more neatly kept than his own, and finally turned and gave Walter another good looking over. "Are these your crew?" he inquired, waving his hand toward the young sailors.

"Yes, sir."

"No men on board?"

"Not one."

"Well, now, I would like to know what you are doing so far from shore in such a boat, and in such weather as this. Are you running away from home?"

"No, sir," replied Walter, emphatically. "Our homes are made so pleasant for us that we wouldn't think of such a thing."

"Perhaps you are lost, then?"

"No, sir. We know just where we are going and what we intend to do. Our vessel is perfectly safe, and this rough weather doesn't trouble us. We're used to it. Shall we stand by to take the provisions aboard?"

It was clear enough to the yacht's company, that the captain would have given something to know what they were doing out there, where they were going, and what their business was, but he made no further attempts to pry into their affairs. The manner in which the yacht was handled when she came alongside his own vessel, and the coolness and confidence manifested by her boy crew, satisfied him that they understood what they were about, and that was as much as he had any right to know. The provisions were quickly hoisted aboard and paid for; and after Walter had cordially thanked the master of the schooner for the favor received at his hands, and the latter had wished Walter a safe run and success in his undertaking, whatever it was, the two vessels parted company—one continuing her voyage toward New Orleans, and the other filling away in pursuit of the smuggler, which was by this time almost hull down.

"Now, fellows, let's turn to and get these things out of the way," said Walter, springing down from the rail, after waving a last farewell to the master of the schooner. "I feel better than I did two hours ago, for, to tell the truth, I was by no means certain that we should meet a vessel; or, if we did, I was afraid she might be commanded by some one who would pay no attention to our request. Suppose we had been knocked about on the Gulf for two or three days, with nothing to eat! Wouldn't we have been in a nice fix? Now, Perk, we've got business for you; and I suggest that you serve us up a cup of hot coffee and a good dinner, with as little delay as possible."

"Now, just listen to me a minute, and I'll tell you what's a fact," replied Perk. "I can't take charge of the galley and act as second in command of the yacht at the same time, so I will resign my lieutenancy in favor of Chase, if you will appoint him."

"Of course I will," said Walter.

"I can't take it, fellows," shouted Chase, from his place at the wheel.

"You've no voice in the matter," replied Eugene. "It is just as the captain says; so consider yourself appointed, and give me your place. It's irregular for an officer to stand a trick at the wheel, you know. That is the duty of us foremast hands."

Of course this was all strategy on Perk's part. The Club knew it, and so did Chase and Wilson; and that was the reason the former remonstrated. After thinking the matter over, however, he decided to act in Perk's place. He told himself that there would be no responsibility attached to the office, for Walter would never leave the deck while that rough weather continued. The young captain regarded his yacht as the apple of his eye; and when he was willing to allow any one even the smallest share in the management of her, it was a sure sign that he liked him and had confidence in him. If Chase had never before been satisfied that the Club were in earnest in all they said, he was now, and so was Wilson.

CHAPTER V.

THE DESERTERS.

BY the aid of the block and tackle which Eugene had rigged over the fore-hatchway, the provisions were lowered through the galley into the hold, where they were stowed away so snugly that they would not be thrown about by the pitching of the vessel. This done, the hatch that led into the hold was closed and fastened. Perk, remembering who had come through there a short time before, put down the hatch himself, stamping it into its place, and securing the bar with the padlock—the fore-hatch was closed and battened down, the block and tackle stowed away in their proper place, and things began to look ship-shape once more.

The foremast hands, as Eugene called himself and companions, who did not hold office, gathered in the standing room to converse; Walter and Chase planked the weather-side of the deck, the former linking his arm through that of his lieutenant, and talking and laughing with him as though they had always been fast friends; a fire was crackling away merrily in the galley stove; and Perk, divested of his coat, his sleeves rolled up to his shoulders, revealing arms as brown and muscular as Uncle Dick's, was superintending the cooking of the "skouse" and "dough-boy," and singing at the top of his voice, the words of an old but favorite song of the Clubs:

"The land of my home is flitting, flitting from my view;
The gale in the sail is setting, toils the merry crew."

He roared out the following lines with more than his usual energy:

"Here let my home be, on the waters wide;
I heed not your anger, for Maggie's by my side.
My own loved Maggie dear, sitting by my side;
Maggie dear, my own love, sitting by my side."

Perk knew a Maggie—only her name was Ella—to whom he used to send valentines and invitations to barbecues and boat-rides, but she was not sitting by his side just then, and consequently we doubt if he would have been quite willing to make his home there on the waters wide, even though he had the yacht for a shelter and the Club for companions. The Maggie of whom Perk was thinking was safe at home in Bellville. She knew that her stalwart admirer was tossing about somewhere on the Gulf, and in spite of her fears for his safety she would have laughed could she have seen him at his present occupation.

"Mind what you are about, Eugene," said Walter, shaking his finger warningly at his brother. "Handle her easy. Perk's in the galley, and that's a guaranty that there's something good coming out of there. If you go to knocking things about and spoiling his arrangements, I'll put you in the brig."

"Very good, Commodore," replied Eugene, touching his hat with mock civility, and giving his trowsers a hitch with one elbow; "I want some of that hot coffee as much as anybody does, sir, even if there is no cream to put in it; and I'll make her ride every wave without a tremble, sir."

Although the young sailors had eaten a hearty lunch not more than three hours before, they were quite ready for dinner, even such a dinner as could be served up out of plain ship's fare. But the principal reason why Perk was ordered below as soon as the provisions were received, was because his services were not then needed on deck, and it was a favorable time to build a fire in the galley while the Gulf was comparatively smooth—that is, the Club thought it comparatively smooth, although a boy unaccustomed to the water would have thought that the yacht was going to roll over and sink out of sight every minute. But the probabilities were that in an hour things would be even worse. The storm that was coming up so slowly and surely promised to be a hard one and a long one; and the dinner that Perk was now serving up might be the last warm meal they would have for a day or two.

Perk's song arose louder and louder, a sure sign that the summons to dinner would not be long delayed. The savory smell of cooking viands came up from below every time the cabin door was opened, and the boys in the standing room snuffed up their noses, said "Ah!" in deep bass voices, and tried to get a glimpse of what was going on in the galley. The jingling of iron rods was heard in the cabin as the table was lowered to its place, then the rattling of dishes, and finally three long-drawn whistles, in imitation of a boatswain's pipe, announced that the meal was ready. Chase, Wilson and Bab answered the call, leaving Walter and his brother to care for the yacht. In half an hour they returned to the deck looking very much pleased and refreshed, and when Perk gave three more whistles Walter and Eugene went below.

"Any orders, captain?" asked Chase, who did not like the idea of being left in charge of the deck even for a minute.

"Follow in the wake of the smuggling vessel," replied Walter. "That's all."

If the sight that greeted Walter's eyes as he went below would have been a pleasing one to a hungry boy under ordinary circumstances, it was doubly so to one who had stood for hours in wet clothing, exposed to the full fury of a cutting north-west wind. The cabin was warm and comfortable, the dishes clean and white, the viands smoking hot, and Walter, Perk and Eugene did ample justice to them. When the meal was finished, the two brothers lent a hand in clearing away the table and washing the dishes; and after the galley stove had been replenished, they, in company with Perk, stretched themselves out on the lee-locker and went to sleep. It seemed to the young captain that he had scarcely closed his eyes when he was aroused by a voice. He started up and saw Bab, whose clothes were dripping with water, lighting the lamps in the cabin.

"Why, it isn't dark, is it?" asked Walter.

"It is growing dark. You've had a glorious sleep, but you had better roll out now and see to things, for poor Chase is in a peck of trouble. It's come."

"What has?"

"Can't you hear it and feel it? Rain and sleet, and wind, and such an ugly, chopping sea. It is coming harder every minute."

That was very evident. The howling of the storm could be plainly heard in the cabin, and the pitching and straining of the yacht as she labored through the waves, told Walter that it was indeed high time he was taking matters into his own hands. Hastily arousing his sleeping companions, he went into the galley for some of his clothing, which he had left there to dry, and in a few minutes, equipped in pea-jacket, gloves, muffler and heavy boots, went up to face the storm. It was already dark, and the rain, freezing as it fell, was coming down in torrents.

"Where's the schooner?" asked Walter.

"I lost sight of her just after I sent Bab down to call you," replied Chase. "My only fear is that we shall not be able to find her again."

"I have no hopes of it," replied Walter. "We'll take an observation to-morrow if the sun comes out, and hold straight for Havana. Call those fellows up from the cabin, and after we've made everything secure, go below and turn in for the night. There's a good fire in the galley."

The crew were quickly summoned to the deck, and in the face of blinding rain and sleet, proceeded to carry out the orders which Walter shouted at them through his trumpet. In twenty minutes more Chase and his drenched companions were enjoying the genial warmth of the galley stove, and the Banner, relieved of the strain upon her, and guided by the hands of her skilful young captain, who stood at the wheel, was riding the waves as gracefully as a sea-gull.

At eight o'clock the boys below, warmed and dried, and refreshed by the pot of hot coffee which the thoughtful Perk had left for them, were sleeping soundly, while Eugene steered the vessel, and Walter and Perk acted as lookouts. But there were other wakeful and active ones on board the Banner, besides Walter and his two companions— some, who, alarmed by the rolling and pitching of the little vessel, and knowing that she was manned only by boys, were making desperate efforts to reach the deck. Had any one been standing in the galley ten minutes after the watch below went into the cabin to sleep, his eyes and ears would have convinced him of this fact. He would have heard a sound like the cutting of wood, and a few seconds afterward he would have seen the point of an auger come up through the floor of the galley, in close proximity to the staple which confined the hatch leading into the hold. Presently he would have seen the auger disappear and come into view again in another place. Then it would have been clear to him that some one in the hold was cutting out the staple by boring holes in a circle around it. Such a proceeding was in reality going on on board the yacht, although the fact was unknown to her crew. Walter had come into the cabin every half hour during his watch to see that everything was safe—looking at the stove, and turning the coats and trowsers that hung before it, so that his companions might have dry clothing to put on when they awoke; but he never thought of casting his eyes toward the hatch.

The auger was kept steadily at work, and presently the plank into which the staple was driven, was cut entirely through, the staple with the circular piece of wood attached was pushed up, the hatch slowly and cautiously raised, and a pair of eyes appeared above the combings and looked through the open door into the cabin. They roved from one to the other of the sleeping boys, and then the hatch was laid carefully back upon the floor of the galley, and a man dressed in the uniform of the revenue service sprang out. Another and another followed, until four of them appeared—all stalwart men, and armed with hatchets, chisels and billets of wood. They halted a moment to hold a whispered consultation, and then, with quick and noiseless footsteps, passed into the cabin. Two of them stopped beside the locker on which Chase and his unconscious companions lay, and the others jerked open the door of the cabin and sprang out into the standing room. Paying no attention to Eugene, who was struck dumb and motionless with astonishment, they glanced about the deck, and discovering Walter and Perk standing on the forecastle, they rushed at them with uplifted weapons.

"Don't move, my lad," said one of the sailors, seizing Perk by the collar, and flourishing a heavy chisel over his head. "If you do, I'll send you straight to Davy's locker."

"Now, just listen to me a minute, and I'll tell you

what's a fact, replied Perk. "Don't trouble yourself to send me there or anywhere else. I am not likely to make much resistance as long as you keep that weapon over me."

Walter was equally cool and collected. Although he was taken completely by surprise by the suddenness of the attack, he had no difficulty in finding an explanation for it. As quick as a flash, some words he had heard a few hours before, came back to him. He remembered that, when he told the captain of the cutter that there were two deserters on board the yacht, the latter had remarked to his lieutenant: "Only two! Then the others must have escaped to the shore." These were the "others" to whom the captain referred. They had not shown themselves, or even made their presence known during the fight in the galley, and their two companions, whom Walter had delivered up to the revenue commander, had not betrayed them. The young captain wished now, when it was too late, that he had searched the hold while the cutter was alongside.

"Easy! easy!" said Walter, when his stalwart assailant seized him by the throat, and brandished his hatchet before his eyes.

7

"Who commands this craft?" demanded the sailor.

"I have the honor," replied Walter, without the least tremor in his voice. "Look here, Mr. Revenue-man," he added, addressing himself to Perk's antagonist, "don't choke that boy. He has no intention of resisting you, and neither have I. We know where you came from, and what you intend to do."

"Well, you're a cool hand!" said Walter's captor, releasing his hold of the young captain's throat, and lowering his hatchet. "You're sensible, too. Will you give the vessel up to us without any fuss?"

"I didn't say so. I've a watch below."

"O, they can't help you, for they're captured already. There's a half a dozen of our fellers down there guarding 'em. Now, look a here, cap'n: there's no use of wasting words over this thing. We're deserters from the United States revenue service, as you know, and we're bound to get to Havana some way or other."

"Well?" said Walter, when the sailor paused.

"Well, we want this vessel to take us there."

"I suppose she will have to do it."

"But there's one difficulty in the way," the sailor went on. "We don't know what course to sail to get there. Do you know anything about navigation?"

"If I didn't, I don't think I should be out here in command of a yacht," said Walter, with a smile. And if he had added that he could take a vessel around the world, he would have told nothing but the truth. He and all the rest of the Club had studied navigation at the Academy, and under Uncle Dick, who drilled them in the use of instruments, and they were quite accomplished navigators for boys of their age.

"Now, this is just the way the thing stands," continued the sailor. "You're too far from Bellville to give us up to the cutter, like you did them other fellers, and we ain't likely to let you turn about and go there either. We're going to Havana; and if you will take us there without any foolishness, we'll be the peaceablest fellers you ever saw. "We'll obey orders, help manage the yacht, live off your grub, and behave ourselves like gentlemen; but if you try to get to windward of us in any way, we'll pitch the last one of you overboard. Mebbe you don't know it, but we are going to ship aboard a Cuban privateer. We can make more that way than we can in Uncle Sam's service—prize-money, you know."

"I know all about it," replied Walter. "I heard it from your captain.

"Well, what do you say?"

"I say, that I will agree to your terms, seeing that I can't help myself. If I could, I might give you a different answer."

"You're sensible. I know you don't want us here, but as we can't get out and walk to Cuba, I'm thinking you will have to put up with our company till we find that privateer."

"O, I didn't agree to any such arrangement," replied Walter, quickly. "I said I would take you to Havana, and so I will; but I am not going all around Robin Hood's barn looking for a Cuban privateer, for I should never find her. There's no such thing in existence. Besides, we've got business of our own to attend to."

"I don't care about your business," said the sailor, who did not know whether to smile or get angry at Walter's plain speech. "You'll go just where we tell you to go. Don't rile us, or you'll find us a desperate lot."

"I don't intend to rile you, and neither am I going to be imposed upon any longer than I can help."

Walter turned on his heel and walked aft, and Perk, taking his cue from the captain's actions, resumed his duties as lookout, paying no more attention to the two sailors than if they had been some of the rope-yarns attached to the rigging. In a few hurried words, Walter explained the state of affairs to Eugene, whom he found almost bursting with impatience to learn the perticulars of the interview on the forecastle, and then looking into the cabin, saw Chase and his companions stretched out on the lockers, wide awake, but afraid to rise for fear of the weapons which the two sailors who were guarding them held over their heads. Walter had been led to believe, by what the sailor said to him, that there were at least eight deserters on board the yacht. Had he known that there were but half that number, he might not have been so ready to accede to their leader's demands.

"Come up out o' that, you revenue men, and let those boys go to sleep," said Walter, in a tone of command.

"Belay your jaw," was the gruff reply. "We

take orders from nobody but Tomlinson. Where is he?"

"Here I am," said the sailor who had held the conversation with Walter. "I've the cap'n's word that we shall be landed in Havana, and no attempts made to humbug us. My name is Tomlinson," he added, turning to the commander of the yacht. "If you want anything out of these fellers, just speak to me. When does the watch below come on deck?"

"As soon as they've had sleep enough. They didn't close their eyes last night."

"All right. I say, mates," continued Tomlinson, addressing his companions in the cabin, "just tumble on to them lockers and go to sleep. You'll be in that watch, and me and Bob'll be in the cap'n's watch; then there'll be two of us on deck all the time."

Walter, without waiting to hear whether the sailor had anything else to say, slammed the door of the cabin, and in no amiable frame of mind went forward and joined Perk; while Tomlinson and his companion, after taking a look at the binnacle, stationed themselves in the waist, where they could see all that was going on.

"Well," said Walter, "what do you think of this?"

"I think that revenue captain must be very stupid to allow six men to desert under his very nose," replied Perk. "If I had been in his place, I would have known every man who belonged to that prize crew; and I could have told whether or not they were all present without mustering them. What are you going to do?"

"I intend to get rid of them at the earliest possible moment. We shall not be able to make Havana in this wind, but we'll hit some port on the Cuban coast, and we'll try to induce these fellows to leave us there. I didn't agree to find a privateer for them, and I am not going to do it. That revenue cutter has been the cause of more trouble to us than she is worth."

And the trouble was not yet ended, if Walter had only known it. The deserters were not to be got rid of as easily as he imagined.

The storm was fully as violent as the young captain expected it would be. It might have been a great deal worse, but if it had been, the story of the Club's adventures would not have been as long as we intend to make it. Walter had ample opportunity for the display of his seamanship, and if any faith is to be put in the word of the deserters, the yacht was well handled. These worthies, true to to their promise, conducted themselves with the utmost propriety. They watched Walter pretty closely for the first few hours, but finding that he knew what he was doing, and that he had no intention of attempting to secure them, they gave themselves no further concern. They obeyed orders as promptly as if Walter had been their lawful captain, and treated the young yachtsmen with a great show of respect.

One day Tomlinson, in reply to a question from Walter, explained their presence on board the yacht. He and five companions belonged to the prize crew which had taken charge of the Banner after her capture by the cutter. While they were guarding the prisoners in the cabin, they learned from them that the yacht was bound for Lost Island, and that she would begin the voyage again as soon as the difficulty with the revenue captain was settled. Upon hearing this, Tomlinson and his friends, who had long been on the lookout for an opportunity to desert the cutter, concealed themselves in the hold, hoping to escape discovery until the Banner was once more outside the harbor of Bellville. They made their first attempt to gain the deck at the wrong time, as it proved, for Perk was on hand to defeat them. They knew that the young sailors had seen but two of their number, and when Walter opened the hatch and ordered them on deck, two of them obeyed, while the others remained behind, awaiting another opportunity to make a strike for their freedom. They never had any intention of taking the vessel out of the hands of her captain. All they wanted was to be on deck where they could see what was going on, and to have the assurance that they should be carried to Havana.

On the morning of the fifth day after leaving Bellville Cuba was in plain sight, and at noon the Banner, after passing several small islands, entered a little harbor about a hundred miles to the eastward of Havana. The Club were in a strange place and among a strange people, but the sight of the little town nestled among the hills was a pleasant one to their eyes. They were heartily tired of being tossed about on the Gulf, and long to feel the solid ground under their feet once more. Their provisions were entirely exhausted, and where the next meal was coming from they had not the slightest idea. This, however, did not trouble them so much as the presence of the deserters. They had quite enough of their company. It was Walter's intention to remain in the harbor until the wind and sea abated, and in the meantime to use every argument he could think of to induce the men to go ashore. The young captain was utterly discouraged. He had seen nothing of the schooner since the first day out, and he was not likely to see her again, for he had been blown a long way out of his course, and by the time he could reach Havana, Fred Craven would be shipped off to Mexico, and the schooner would have discharged her contraband cargo and be half way on her return voyage to Bellville.

"Captain, there's an officer wants to come aboard," said Tomlinson, breaking in upon his reverie.

Walter looked toward the shore and saw a boat putting off from the nearest wharf, and a man dressed in uniform standing in the stern waving his handkerchief. "Who is he?" asked the young captain.

"One of them revenue fellers, I guess. These chaps are very particular."

"I am glad to hear it, for if we can find that

schooner we may be able to induce them to examine her."

The yacht was thrown up into the wind, and in a few minutes the officer came on board—a fierce-looking Spaniard, with a mustache which covered all the lower part of his face, and an air as pompous as that of the revenue captain. He touched his hat to Walter, and addressed some words to him which the latter could not understand.

"I hope there's nothing wrong," said the commander, anxiously. "I may have violated some of the rules of the port, for I am like a cat in a strange garret here. Tomlinson, can you speak his lingo?"

"No, sir. Talk French to the lubber, if you can."

Walter could and did. The visitor replied in the same language, and his business was quickly settled. He was a revenue officer, as Tomlinson had surmised, and wanted to look at the yacht's papers, which were quickly produced; although of what use they could be to a man who did not understand English, Walter could not determine. The officer looked at them a moment, with an air of profound wisdom, and then returning them with the remark that they were all right, touched his hat and sprang into his boat. As soon as he was clear of the side the yacht filled away again, Walter taking his stand upon the rail and looking out for a convenient place to moor his vessel; but there were but two small wharves in the harbor, and every berth seemed to be occupied. As he ran his eye along the brigs, barks and schooners, wondering if there were an American among them, his gaze suddenly became fastened upon a little craft which looked familiar to him. He was certain he had seen that black hull and those tall, raking masts before. He looked again, and in a voice which trembled in spite of all his efforts to control it, requested Eugene to hand him his glass.

"What's the matter?" asked the crew in concert, crowding up to the rail. "What do you see?"

"He sees the Stella, and so do I!" exclaimed Bab, in great excitement.

"Yes, it is the Stella," said Walter, so overjoyed at this streak of good fortune that he could scarcely speak. "Now, we'll see if these Cuban revenue officers are as worthless as some of our own. But I say, Perk," he added, his excitement suddenly increasing, "take this glass and tell me who those three persons are who are walking up the hill, just beyond the schooner."

Perk leveled the glass, but had not held it to his eye long before his hand began to tremble, and his face assumed an expression much like that it had worn during his contest with the deserters, and while he was confronting Bayard Bell and his crowd. Without saying a word he handed the glass to Eugene, and settling his hat firmly on his head pushed back his coat sleeves. He acted as if he wanted to fight.

"They are Mr. Bell, the captain of the Stella, and—who is that walking between them? Fred Craven, as I live!" Eugene almost shouted.

"Now, listen to me a minute, and I'll tell you what's a fact," said Perk, bringing his clenched fist down into the palm of his hand. "That's just who they are."

"Fred sees us, too," continued Eugene. "He is looking back at us."

"I didn't think I could be mistaken," said Walter. "Perk, keep your eye on them and see where they go. Stand by, fellows. When we reach the wharf make everything fast as soon as possible; and Eugene, you and Bab see if you can find that revenue officer. If you do, tell him the whole story, and take him on board the schooner. Perk and I will follow Fred, and Chase and Wilson will watch the yacht.

In ten minutes more, the Banner's bow touched a brig lying alongside the wharf, and too impatient to wait until she was made fast, Walter and Perk hurried to the shore and ran up the hill in pursuit of Fred Craven. How great would have been their astonishment, had they known that they were running into a trap that had been prepared for them

CHAPTER VI.

A CHAPTER OF INCIDENTS.

AS soon as the yacht had been made fast to the brig, Eugene and Bab sprang over the rail and hurried away in search of the revenue officer, leaving Chase and Wilson to put everything to rights, and to look out for the vessel. The latter, excited and delighted almost beyond measure at the prospect of the speedy rescue of Fred Craven, kept their eyes fastened upon Walter and Perk, as they ran up the hill, and when they disappeared from view, reluctantly set to work to furl the sails and clear up the deck. The deserters, however, suddenly seemed to have lost all interest in the yacht. Instead of assisting the young sailors at their work, they gathered in the standing-room and held a whispered consultation, ever and anon glancing toward the lieutenant, to make sure that he was not listening or observing their movements. Chase did not appear to notice what was going on, but for all that he was wide awake. Feeling the full weight of the responsibility that Walter had thrown upon him, in leaving him in charge of the yacht, he was inclined to be nervous and suspicious of everything.

"What are those fellows up to?" he asked of his companion, in a whisper.

"What makes you think they are up to anything?" inquired Wilson.

"I judge by their actions. If they are not planning some mischief, why do they watch us so closely, and talk in so low a tone that we cannot hear them? How easy it would be for them to take the yacht from us and go to sea again, if they felt so inclined! I really believe that is what they are talking about."

"I never thought of that," said Wilson, almost paralyzed at the simple mention of the thing. "What would Walter say if some such misfortune should befall the Banner, while she is under our charge? He would never forgive us. But of course, they won't attempt it, for they don't understand navigation."

But Wilson was not as well acquainted with the dispositions of the men with whom they had to deal as Chase was. The latter had made a shrewd guess, for the deserters were at that very moment discussing a plan for seizing the Banner and making off with her. They lived in constant fear of capture—they did not know at what instant they might see the revenue cutter coming into the harbor—and they could not feel free from danger until they were safe on board the privateer of which they were in search. They wanted to go to Havana at once, and this forced delay was more than they could endure. The leader of the deserters was urging an immediate departure, but his companions were not quite ready to give their consent to his plans.

"Perhaps we shall now find out what they are talking about," whispered Chase, suddenly, "for here comes Tomlinson. Keep your weather-eye open, and be ready for any tricks."

"I say, lads!" exclaimed the deserter, approaching the place where the boys were at work, "what's your business here, anyhow? What brought you to Cuba?"

"Didn't the captain tell you?" asked Chase.

"He didn't even hint it."

"Then it isn't worth while to make inquiries of us. Our business concerns no one but ourselves and our friends."

8

"Well, ain't me and my mates friends of yours? Mebbe we can help you."

"If the captain had thought so, no doubt he would have taken you into his confidence. Wait until he returns, and talk to him."

"Where has he gone?"

"I don't know."

"When will he be back?"

"I haven't the slightest idea."

"How long before he is going to sail for Havana?"

"I don't know that either. He'll not start until this wind goes down and he gets some provisions—perhaps not even then. His business may keep him here a week."

Tomlinson turned on his heel, and walking aft, joined his companions. "It must be done, mates," said he in a whisper. "The lads are as dumb as tar-buckets, and all I could find out was that the yacht may stay here several days. During that time, the privateer may make up her crew and go to sea, and we shall be left out in the cold. We ought to be in Havana now."

"But I am 'most afraid to trust you in command,

Tom," said one of the deserters. "The captain says it is a good hundred miles to Havana."

"No matter if it is a thousand; I can find it. All we have to do is to sail along the coast. We'll know the city when we see it, won't we?"

"But we need some grub, and how are we going to get it?"

"As soon as it grows dark we'll land and steal some—that's the way we'll get it. What do you say now? I am going to Havana in this yacht: who's going with me?"

This question settled the matter at once. All the deserters were anxious to find the privateer, and since Tomlinson, who was the ruling spirit of the band, was determined to start in search of her, the others, rather than be left behind, decided to accompany him, and run all the risks of shipwreck.

The immediate seizure of the yacht having been resolved upon, the next question to be settled was: What should be done with the boys? After a few minutes' conversation on this point, Tomlinson and two of his companions went forward to assist Chase and Wilson, while the fourth walked to the stern, and leaning his folded arms upon the rail, gazed listlessly into the water. Tomlinson and his two friends lent effective aid, and the deck of the Banner soon began to present its usual scene of neatness and order. The former kept up a running fire of jokes and stories, in the midst of which he suddenly paused, and stood fiercely regarding his companion in the standing room.

"Bob," said he, in a tone of command, "I never knew before that you were a soger. Look around and find something to do."

"Where shall I go?" asked Bob, gruffly.

"Anywhere, so long as you don't stand there skulking. Go into the cabin, and put it in order against the captain comes back."

Bob slowly straightened up and sauntered down the companion-ladder, but almost immediately reappeared. "The cabin's all right," he growled. "Everything's in order."

"Then go into the galley, or into the hold, and see if things are all right there," returned Tomlinson, angrily. "I know you can find something to do somewhere about the yacht."

Bob disappeared in the cabin again, and presently Chase heard him tumbling things about in the hold. In a few minutes he once more thrust his head out of the companion-way.

"Well, what's the row now?" asked Tomlinson. "Find anything to do down there?"

"Plenty of it," was the reply. "Lieutenant, will you step down here a moment?"

Chase, believing from Bob's tone and manner, that he had found something very much out of the way in the hold, started toward the companion-way; but just before he reached it, a thought struck him, and he stopped and looked earnestly at the man. "What's the matter down there?" he asked.

"One of the water-butts has sprung a leak, sir," said the sailor.

"That's a dreadful calamity, isn't it? Don't you know what to do in such a case? Bail the water out of the leaky butt into one of the others."

"But there's none to bail out, sir. Every drop has leaked out, and the water is ankle deep all over the hold."

"Wilson," said Chase, turning to his companion, "just give a stroke or two on that pump, will you?"

Wilson did as he was requested, but not a drop of water was brought up. The Banner's hold was as dry as a piece of hard-tack.

"How are you, leaky water-butt!" exclaimed

Chase, with a significant glance at Wilson. "Anything else wrong below, Bob?"

The sailor, somewhat disconcerted, did not know what to say at first, but after a look at Tomlinson, he replied:

"Yes, sir. Everything is pitched out of place, and I shall need some one to help me put 'em to rights. I can't lift those heavy tool-chests by myself."

"Look here, Bob," said Chase, suddenly; "you're not a good hand at this business. You can't tell a falsehood and keep a straight face."

"Falsehood, sir!" exclaimed the sailor, ascending a step or two nearer the top of the companion-ladder, as if he had half a mind to come on deck and resent the word. "Do you say I lie?"

"Well, no; I didn't say so," replied Chase, not in the least intimidated by the man's threatening glances; "I can generally express myself without being so rude. But that is just what I mean. You know the hold is in order, and so do I; for I was down there not five minutes before we landed. I am too old to be taken in by any such flimsy trick as this. You'll have to study up a better one if you expect to deceive me."

So saying, Chase walked back to the forecastle and resumed his work, while Bob, not knowing what reply to make, went down into the cabin. The lieutenant kept his eye upon Tomlinson and his two friends, and saw that, when they thought themselves unobserved, they exchanged glances indicative of rage and disappointment. One by one they walked aft to the standing room, and in a few minutes more were holding another council of war.

".Chase, you're a sharp one," said Wilson, approvingly. "If I had been in your place I should have been nicely fooled. What do you suppose they want to do?"

"They intend to capture us and run off with the yacht; that's their game. They are afraid to lay hands on us as long as we remain on deck, but if they could get us into the cabin out of sight, they would make prisoners of us in a hurry. O, there's nothing to be afraid of," added Chase, noticing the expression of anxiety that settled on his companion's face. "If they attack us we'll summon help from this brig."

The deserters were much astonished as well as disheartened by the failure of their clumsy attempt to entice the lieutenant into the hold. They saw that he suspected them and was on the alert. They were none the less determined, however, to possess themselves of the yacht, and when they gathered in the standing room Tomlinson, who was fruitful in expedients, had another plan to propose. While they were discussing it a sailor, who had for some time been leaning over the brig's rail, watching all that was going on on board the Banner, swung himself off by his hands and dropped upon her deck. Chase and Wilson saw him, but supposing that he was one of the crew of the brig, whose curiosity had prompted him to visit the yacht, they said nothing to him.

The stranger, finding that no one paid any attention to his movements, set himself at work to examine the yacht very closely, especially as much of her internal arrangements as he could see through her hatchways. He spent ten minutes in this way, and then sauntered toward the standing room. The sound of his footsteps attracted the attention of Tomlinson, who looked up and greeted him with:

"Hallo, mate! Do you happen to have a pipeful of tobacco about you?"

The sailor produced a good-sized plug from his

pocket and asked, as he handed it to Tomlinson: "What craft is this?"

"She's a private yacht—the Banner—and belongs in Bellville, Louisiana," was the answer. "Me and my mates here are the crew. We are hired by the year, and all we have to do is to take a half a dozen young gentlemen wherever they want to go."

"You have papers, of course?"

"Yes. The captain keeps them in that desk in the cabin."

The stranger directed his gaze down the companion-way, and after taking a good look at the little writing-desk Tomlinson pointed out to him, asked, as he jerked his thumb over his shoulder toward the two boys on the forecastle:

"Who are those fellows? I think I have seen them somewhere."

"Their names are Chase and Wilson, and they are a couple of green hands who came out with us. The cap'n and steward have gone ashore to get some grub. We've been knocked about on the Gulf for the last five days, and we've made way with the last mouthful of salt horse and hard tack. We haven't had any breakfast yet."

"You haven't!" exclaimed the sailor. "Then

come with me. I am mate of the schooner Stella, which lies a little way below here. I'll give you a good breakfast and a pipe to smoke after it."

Tomlinson and his friends were much too hungry to decline an invitation of this kind. Without saying a word they followed the mate on board the brig, thence to the wharf, and in a few minutes found themselves on board the Stella. After conducting them into the forecastle, their guide made his way across the deck and down the companion-ladder into the cabin, where he found Mr. Bell pacing to and fro.

"Well," said the latter, pausing in his walk, "waste no time in words now. Have you succeeded?"

"Not yet, sir," replied the mate. "I found more men there than I expected to find—four sailors, who say they are the hired crew of the yacht, but I know they are deserters from Uncle Sam's revenue service. How they came on board the Banner, I did not stop to inquire. They told me they had eaten no breakfast, and I brought them up here. We can easily keep them out of the way until the work is done."

"Very good," said Mr. Bell. "Tell the steward

to serve them up a good meal at once. Was there anybody else on board the yacht?"

"Yes, sir; Chase and Wilson were there, and I am now going back to attend to them. The vessel's papers are kept in a writing-desk in the cabin, and I shall have no trouble in securing them."

The mate left the cabin, and after repeating Mr. Bell's order to the steward, sprang over the rail, and hurried along the wharf toward the place where the Banner lay. When he arrived within sight of her, he was surprised to see that Chase and Wilson were making preparations to get under way. The jib was already shaking in the wind, and the foresail was slowly crawling up the mast. Chase was determined that the deserters should not return on board the yacht if he could prevent it. He would anchor the vessel at a safe distance from the shore, with the sails hoisted, and if Tomlinson and his friends attempted to reach her by the aid of a boat he would slip the cable and run away from them.

"It seems that I am just in time," soliloquized the mate of the Stella. "A few minutes' delay would have spoiled everything. Tony," he added in Spanish, turning to a negro who stood close by, and who seemed to be awaiting his orders, "here's the note and here's the money. Be in a hurry now, and mind what you are about."

The negro took the articles the mate handed him, and after putting the money into his pocket, and stowing the letter away in the crown of his hat, he sprang on board the brig and made his way toward the yacht; while the mate concealed himself behind some sugar hogsheads that stood on the wharf to observe his movements. He saw the negro drop down upon the deck of the Banner and present the note to Chase, and he noticed too the excitement it produced upon the two boys.

The note the lieutenant received was as follows:

"Friend CHASE:

We have come up with Featherweight at last. He is still in the hands of the smugglers, but with a little assistance, we can easily rescue him. Come immediately, and bring all the boys with you. This darkey will act as your guide.

      In great haste,
        WALTER."

"That's business,," cried Chase, thrusting the note into his pocket, and bustling about in such a state of excitement that he scarcely knew what to do first. "We'll see fun now. Close those hatches, and we'll be off. I only hope I shall get a chance to do something for Fred Craven. I want to show him that I don't forget favors."

"Must we leave the Banner to take care of herself?" asked Wilson.

"What else can we do? We can't very well put her into our pockets and take her with us."

"But what if something should happen to her? Suppose the deserters should return and run off with her?"

"That's Walter's lookout, and not ours," replied Chase, locking the door of the cabin, and putting the key into his pocket. "I wonder if this fellow can tell us where the captain is, and what he is doing? Can you speak English?" he added, addressing the negro.

The man stared at him, but made no answer.

"Can you talk French?" continued Chase, speaking in that language.

The negro grinned, but said nothing.

"Well, we can't talk Spanish, so we must wait until we see Walter, before we can find out what has been going on," said Wilson. "But it seems strange that he should ask us to come to him and leave the vessel with no one to watch her, doesn't it?"

"Under ordinary circumstances it would," answered Chase, springing upon the deck of the brig, and hurrying toward the wharf. "But Walter is working for Fred Craven, you know, and he would rather lose a dozen yachts, if he had them, than to allow a hair of his head to be harmed."

When the boys reached the wharf they put themselves under the guidance of the negro, who led them through an arched gateway to the street, where stood a heavy cotton wagon, to which was attached a team of four mules. At a sign from the negro, the young sailors sprang into the vehicle, and the man mounting one of the mules, set up a shout, the team broke into a gallop, and the boys were whirled rapidly down the street.

When the wagon had disappeared, the mate of the Stella arose from his place of concealment behind the sugar hogsheads, and with a smile of satisfaction on his face walked rapidly toward his vessel. He spent a few minutes in the cabin with Mr. Bell, and when he came on deck, ordered the yawl to be manned. While this command was being obeyed by a part of the schooner's company, the others busied themselves in bringing boxes and bales up from the cabin; and when the yawl was hauled alongside, these articles were handed down to her crew, who stowed them away under the thwarts. This done, the mate took his seat at the helm, the crew gave way on the oars, and presently the yawl was lying alongside Walter Gaylord's yacht. The mate at once boarded her; the fore-hatch, which Chase and Wilson, in their haste to obey the order contained in Walter's note, had neglected to fasten, was opened, and the officer and two of his men jumped down into the galley, whence they made their way into the hold. The boxes and bales were then passed up out of the yawl and through the hatches, one by one, and stowed away behind the water-butts. This much being accomplished, the mate came up out of the hold, and leaving his men to close the hatch, went into the cabin and opened the desk which Tomlinson had pointed out to him. Almost the first thing his eyes rested upon was an official envelope, addressed to "Captain Walter Gaylord, Commanding the Yacht Banner." Thrusting it hastily into his pocket, he ascended to the deck, and in a few seconds more the yawl was on her way down the harbor. Arriving alongside the

Stella, the mate once more sought an interview with Mr. Bell, and handed him the envelope he had taken from Walter's desk. The gentleman glanced quickly over the document it contained, and then tearing it into fragments, walked to one of the stern windows and threw the pieces into the water.

"There!" said he, in a tone of exultation. "The next time Captain Gaylord is asked to produce his clearance papers, I think he will have some trouble in finding them. Before he is done with us he will wish he had stayed at home where he belongs."

CHAPTER VII.

DON CASPER.

MANY were the speculations in which Chase and Wilson indulged, as they were whirled along over the rough road, and bumped about from one side to the other of the cotton wagon. What sort of a situation was Featherweight in? Where had Walter and Perk found the wagon; and how had they made the negro understand the service required of him, seeing that the man could speak neither English nor French, and the captain and his companion could not talk Spanish? These, and a multitude of questions of like character, occupied the minds of the boy-tars for the next half hour, and during that time, they left the village more than five miles behind them; but still they were whirled along without the least diminution of speed, the negro swinging his whip and yelling with all the power of his lungs, and the heavy wagon rolling and plunging in a way that reminded the young sailors of the antics the Banner had performed during her voyage across the Gulf.

"There's one thing about it"—shouted Wilson, holding fast to the side of the vehicle, and speaking in a very loud tone of voice, in order to make himself heard—"if Walter told this darkey to drive fast, he is obeying orders most faithfully. Where do you suppose he is taking us? And tell me, if you can, how Walter and Perk could have got so far out into the country, during the hour and a half they have been gone from the vessel?"

"That is the very question that was passing through my own mind," said Chase. "To tell the truth, there's something about this business that doesn't look exactly right."

"Well, you needn't mind knocking my brains out, if it doesn't look exactly right," roared Wilson, as a sudden lurch of the wagon brought his friend's head in violent contact with his own. "Keep on your side if you can, Chase."

The loud rumbling of the wheels, and the rocking and swaying of the clumsy vehicle as it flew over the uneven road, proved an effectual check to conversation. The boys clung to opposite sides of the wagon, noting the different objects of interest as they sped along, and wondering what was to be the end of this adventure. Every mile of the way, they saw something to remind them that Cuba was in a state of insurrection. Groups of excited men were gathered in front of every plantation house they passed, and now and then they met squads of government patrols riding leisurely along the road. The officers of these squads all looked suspiciously at the boys, as they dashed by, and one, in particular, bent such savage glances upon them, that they were glad when he had passed out of sight.

"I say, Wilson," shouted Chase, suddenly, "do you know that the expression on that officer's face, has set me to thinking?"

"I don't doubt it," yelled Wilson, in reply. "It set me to thinking, too. Wouldn't it have been a joke on us, if he had taken us for spies or something, and arrested us?"

"I confess, I can't see where the joke would come in. How could we ever get out of a scrape of that kind? We are in a strange country, among people who speak a language different from ours, and we haven't a friend within seven or eight hundred miles. It would be a serious matter for us, the first thing you know. I am glad that fierce-looking fellow is out of sight, and I hope we shall not meet another like him."

If the boys had known what the officers did in less than five minutes after they met him, they might not have felt so very much relieved after all. He rode straight ahead, until a bend in the road concealed him from view, and then suddenly halting his squad, addressed a few words to two of his men, who wheeled their horses and galloped back in pursuit of the young sailors. They rode just fast enough to keep the wagon in sight, and when they saw it draw up at the door of a plantation house, they faced about again and hurried back to their companions. They must have had some exciting report to make, for when their officer heard it, he ordered his men into their saddles, and led them down the road at a rapid gallop.

When the negro driver reined his mules through a wide gateway, and drew up in front of the door of the house of which we have spoken, the boys knew that their ride was ended. They were glad of it, for it was anything but pleasant to be jolted and bumped about over such roads as those they had just traversed. They jumped out when the wagon stopped, and after stretching their arms and legs, and knocking the dust out of their hats, looked about them with interest. They saw before them a large and comfortable plantation house, situated in a little grove of oleanders and orange trees, flanked by neat negro quarters, and surrounded by extensive sugar-fields, which stretched away on every side. They looked around for Walter and Perk, but could see nothing of them. They were not allowed much time for making observations, however, for the moment the wagon stopped, a portly foreign-looking gentleman, whom the boys at once put down as the proprietor of the plantation, made his appearance at the door. He looked curiously at his visitors, and while the latter were wondering what they ought to say to him, the negro driver mounted the steps, and taking a letter from the crown of his hat, handed it to his master. The reading of the document had an astonishing effect upon the man. He opened his eyes to their widest extent, and muttering something in Spanish, hurried down the steps, and seized each of the boys by the hand.

"Come in! come in!" said he, hurriedly, and in tolerable English. "I am delighted to see you, but I am surprised that Captain Conway should have sent you out here in the day time. Come in, before the patrols see you."

Chase and Wilson looked inquiringly at one another. "Captain Conway!" whispered the latter, as he and his companion followed the gentleman up the steps. "If *he* had any hand in sending us here, we are in a scrape, as sure as we're a foot high."

"I would give something to know what is in that letter," said Chase. "Where are Walter and Perk?"

"Haven't the slightest idea; but I know that we shall not find them here. The chances are ten to one that we shall never see them again. If there were not so many negroes standing around, I would take to my heels in short order."

Chase was bewildered and perplexed beyond measure. The simple mention of the name of the captain of the Stella, had aroused a thousand fears in his mind; and imagining that all sorts of dreadful things were about to happen to him, he was more than half inclined to spring off the steps and make a desperate dash for his freedom, in spite of the presence of the negroes; but while he was thinking about it, the foreign-looking gentleman conducted him and his companion through the hall and into a room, the door of which he was careful to close and lock behind him. The two boys watched his movements with a good deal of anxiety, and while Wilson glanced toward the open window, Chase stepped forward and confronted the man.

"I am afraid," said he, "that there is some mistake here, Mr.——Mr.——"

"Don Casper Nevis," said the gentleman, supplying the name. "There is no mistake whatever.'

"But where is the captain?" continued Chase "we expected to find him here."

"O, he'll not come until dark; and he ought not to have sent you out here in broad daylight, when he knows that every mile of the road is guarded. Where is the schooner?"

"We left her at the wharf."

"She ought to be up here. These Spanish officers are getting to be very strict lately, and it is a wonder they didn't search her the moment she landed. I understand that both you and your vessel are known and suspected. You must be very cautious. Your safest plan would be to go back to town, and have the schooner brought into the bay at the rear of my plantation. I have boats there, and everything in readiness."

"But, Don," replied Chase, "I don't see the necessity for so much secrecy."

"My young friend, you don't understand the matter at all," said Don Casper with a smile. "But you are weary with travel, and we will say no more about it, until you have refreshed yourselves. We shall have ample time to make all the arrangements after you have drank a cup of chocolate and eaten a piece of toast."

As the Don said this, he unlocked the door and went out, leaving the boys to themselves.

"Didn't I tell you that this thing didn't look just right?" demanded Chase, in an excited whisper. "That darkey has made a mistake, and brought us to the wrong house."

"But how in the name of sense could he do that?" asked Wilson, utterly confounded. "He must have known where Walter was when he gave him that note. By the way, let me look at it a moment."

Chase handed out the letter, and was more amazed and alarmed than ever by the expression that settled on his friend's face as he ran his eye over the missive. "What's the matter now?" he asked. "Anything else wrong?"

"Nothing much," was the answer; "only that's not Walter Gaylord's writing—that's all."

"Eh!" exclaimed Chase, jumping from his chair.

"O, it is the truth, as you will find out when you meet Walter again. I can tell his writing as far as I can see it."

"Then who wrote this letter?"

"I wish I knew. Somebody has humbugged us very nicely, and I believe that Captain Conway and Mr. Bell are at the bottom of it."

"Let's jump out of this window and make the best of our way back to town," exclaimed Chase, almost beside himself with excitement and terror. "There's no knowing what this old Creole intends to do to us."

"And there's no knowing what may happen to the Banner in our absence. What if those deserters should run off with her? Here we are in Cuba, without a cent in our pockets, and if we should lose the yacht how would we ever get home?"

"Gracious!" exclaimed Chase.

"I'll jump out of the window and run if you will," continued Wilson.

With a common impulse the two boys arose from their seats and moved across the floor on tiptoe; but just as Chase placed his hands on the window-sill preparatory to springing out, the door suddenly opened, and three negroes came in—one bringing a small table, and each of the others carrying a tray filled with dishes and eatables on his head. So sudden was their entrance that the boys did not have time to retreat to their chairs, and Chase remained standing with his hands on the window-sill, gazing steadily out into the sugar-field as if he saw something there that interested him very much, while Wilson, with his hands clasped behind his back, and his head turned on one side, appeared to be lost in admiration of a picture that hung on the wall.

The boys stood in these positions until they were aroused by a tap on the shoulder. They turned to find themselves alone with one of the negroes, and to see the table spread in front of a window, and loaded with a most tempting display of viands. They did not wait for a second invitation. They had taken no breakfast; there was no knowing when and where they would obtain another meal; and there was no reason why they should go hungry even if they were in trouble. No one, to have seen them at the table, would have imagined that they were under any apprehensions of danger, for the way the eggs and toast disappeared was wonderful; but in the midst of their enjoyment, and before their appetites were half appeased, the door was suddenly thrown open and Don Casper entered pale and breathless.

"The patrol!" he almost gasped. "It is just as I feared it would be. You have been seen and followed, and if you are found here, I am ruined. No time is to be lost. Come with me immediately."

The man spoke so hurriedly and brokenly that the boys could not understand all he said, and consequently they were at a loss to determine what the danger was that threatened them. But the expression on the face of their host warned them that there was something amiss; and without stopping to ask questions, they caught up their hats and followed him from the room. As they were hurrying along the hall, they glanced toward the gate and, through a dense cloud of dust, raised by a multitude of horses' hoofs, they caught a partial glimpse of a squadron of troopers who were galloping into the yard. And these were not the only soldiers upon the premises, as they found when they reached the door which opened upon the back verandah. There was another squad of cavalrymen approaching along the lane that led to the negro quarters. The house was surrounded.

"Gracias á Dios!" ejaculated the Don, turning ghastly pale.

"What's the matter?" asked Wilson, innocently. "We have done nothing wrong, and we are not afraid of the patrols."

"Nothing wrong!" the Don almost shrieked. "Is it nothing to smuggle cases of arms into a country in a state of rebellion?"

"Cases of arms!" repeated Chase.

"Smuggle!" echoed Wilson. "We know a smuggler, but we never ——"

"Don't stop to talk," interrupted the Don, almost fiercely; and as he spoke he seized the boys by their arms, and dragged them along the hall and down a flight of rickety steps that led into the cellar. Chase and Wilson, more perplexed than ever, tried to gain his ear for a moment, but he seemed all of a sudden to have been struck both deaf and dumb, for he would say nothing or listen to nothing, but hurried them along through utter darkness, and finally, after giving them both a strong push, released his hold of them. A moment afterward the boys heard a door softly closed behind them, and a key turned in a lock. Filled with consternation, they stood for a few seconds speechless and motionless, listening intently, and afraid to move for fear of coming in contact with something in the darkness. Chase was the first to break the silence.

"Well, this beats all the scrapes I ever got into," said he. "Do you begin to see through it yet?"

"I believe I do," replied Wilson. "The last words that old Creole uttered, explain the matter clearly. He takes us for smugglers, and imagines that we have come here with a cargo of small-arms."

"How did he get that impression?" asked Chase, who wanted to see how far his friend's opinions coincided with his own.

"Through the note that negro gave him."

"Who wrote that note?"

"Mr. Bell. He saw us come into the harbor, and he would have been dull indeed if he could not guess what brought us there. He and his crew have set themselves at work to outwit us, as they outwitted the revenue captain in the Cove."

"And they have accomplished their object, and

got us into a pretty mess besides. They are altogether too smart for us. What's that?"

The tramping of feet, the rattling of sabres, and the jingling of spurs sounded from the rooms overhead, telling them that the soldiers had arrived and were searching the house. Backward and forward passed the heavy footsteps, and presently they were heard upon the cellar stairs. The boys listened with curiosity rather than fear, and by the sounds which came to them from the cellar could tell pretty nearly what the soldiers were doing. They heard them talking to one another, and overturning boxes and barrels, and they knew too when the search was abandoned, and the soldiers returned to the room above.

The young tars did not breathe any easier after they were gone, for they were not in the least frightened by the proximity of the Spanish troopers. They were not smugglers, and they could prove the fact to anybody's satisfaction. They almost wished they had not permitted the Don to conceal them, for that of itself looked like a confession of guilt, and might be used as evidence against them in case they were captured. The papers, which were safely stowed away in Walter's desk in the cabin of the

Banner, would show who they were and where they came from, and a few minutes' examination of the yacht would prove that there were no small-arms on board of her. The boys thought of all these things, and waited impatiently for the Don to come and release them. They wanted to explain matters to him, if they could by any possibility induce him to listen.

For fully half an hour the troopers continued to search the house, and at the end of that time, having satisfied themselves that the boys were beyond their reach, they mounted their horses and galloped out of the yard. The young sailors now became more impatient than ever for the Don to make his appearance, but they waited in vain. They held their breath and listened, but could not hear a single footstep. The house was as silent as if it had been deserted. As the hours dragged slowly by without bringing any one to their relief, the boys became harassed by a new fear, and that was that the master of the plantation did not intend to release them—that he was keeping them locked up for some purpose of his own. Filled with dismay at the thought, they arose from the boxes on which they had seated themselves, and began moving cautiously about their prison with extended arms. A few minutes' examination of the apartment showed them that it was a wine-cellar, for there were shelves on three sides of it, which were filled with bottles. On the fourth side was the door, and that was the only opening in the walls. There was no window to be found, nor even a crevice large enough to admit a ray of light. There was no way of escape. Wilson, determined to make the best of the matter, kept up a tolerably brave heart, but Chase, as was usual with him when in trouble, became despondent.

"We're here," said he, in a gloomy voice, "and here we may remain for the term of our natural lives, for all we know. If Mr. Bell wrote that note which we thought came from Walter, I know what object he had in view. This Don Casper is a friend of his, and now that he has got us in his power, he is going to hold fast to us."

"He won't if he gives us the least chance for our liberty," said Wilson, striving to keep up his friend's courage. "But things may not be as bad as you think."

"They are bad enough, are they not? To be thrown as we were, under the most suspicious circumstances, into the hands of a man we never saw before, who, without condescending to give us an intelligible explanation of the motive that prompts his actions, shuts us up in a dark cellar, and walks off with the key in his pocket, to be gone nobody knows how long—that is bad enough, but there may be worse things yet to come. Do you know that we are in a country in which a terrible war is being carried on?"

"I do."

"And that both sides are treating their prisoners with the greatest cruelty; in some cases shooting them?"

"Certainly. Having read the papers, I am not likely to be ignorant of the fact."

"Well, now, did it ever strike you that we— Eh? You know," said Chase, unable to give utterance to the fears that just then passed through his mind.

"No," replied Wilson; "it never did."

"It has struck me that some such thing might happen to us," continued Chase, in a trembling voice. "This Creole is a rebel, and thinks we are friends of his. The Spaniards think so too, for they have searched the house with the intention of

10

capturing us. If we had fallen into their hands, might they not have put an end to us without giving us an opportunity to say a word in our defence, believing as they do that we are friends of the Cubans?"

"It is possible," replied Wilson, coolly.

"Gracious! If I had thought of all these things, I never would have had anything to do with this expedition, I tell you. How would I look, set up against a brick wall, with half a dozen Spaniards standing in front of me, ready to shoot me down at the word? I wish I had stayed on Lost Island and starved there." And Chase, terrified almost beyond measure by the picture he had drawn, jumped to his feet, hurried off through the darkness, and bumped his head severely against the solid oak planks which formed the door of their prison.

"You are not set up against a brick wall yet, at all events," said Wilson, laughing, in spite of himself. "Don't take on so, old fellow, or I shall believe you are in a fair way to become a coward. Here's a dry-goods box. Let's lie down on it and try to get a wink of sleep."

"Sleep!" groaned Chase, holding one hand to

his head, and with the other feeling his way through the darkness, in the direction from which his companion's voice sounded; "how can you think of such a thing? Don't lie there so still. Wake up and talk to me."

It was not possible that Chase could ever become a greater coward than he was at that moment, and he told himself so. The thought that he was in a strange country, surrounded by men who were in arms against one another, and that some of them—perhaps the very ones who had perpetrated the cruelties of which he had read in the papers—had been in that very house searching for him, was dreadful. It tested his fortitude to the very utmost. Even the darkness which filled the wine-cellar had terrors for him, and he hardly dared to move a finger, for fear it might come in contact with some living thing. For three long hours he sat upon his box, in a state of terror beyond our power to describe, and all this while, the plucky Wilson, with a happy indifference to circumstances, which Chase greatly envied, slumbered heavily.

CHAPTER VIII.

CHASE RISES TO EXPLAIN.

WILSON knew, as well as Chase, that the latter had not overestimated the dangers of their situation. Cuba was in a state of insurrection, having declared her independence of Spain. Several battles had been fought between the rebels and the Spanish troops, and deeds of violence were daily enacted in every part of the island. Wilson knew all this before the voyage for Cuba was commenced, but he had never dreamed that he and the rest of the crew of the yacht could in any way become mixed up in the troubles. He had set out simply with the intention of assisting to rescue Fred Craven from the power of the smugglers, and here he was suspected of being a smuggler himself, and of having in his possession cases of arms to be delivered to the agents of the Cuban government. Don Casper, to whose house he had been brought in so strange a manner, thought that such was his occupation and character, for he had said so; and he had also hinted that the Spanish troopers suspected them, and that it would be dangerous to fall into their hands. This was certainly an unlooked for termination to the expedition upon which he and the members of the Sportsman's Club had entered with so much eagerness, and it was enough to awaken in his mind the most serious misgivings. But he was a courageous fellow, and knowing that much depended upon keeping up the spirits of his desponding friend, he affected an indifference that he was very far from feeling. He slept because he was utterly exhausted by the labor and excitement he had undergone during the last few days.

Chase was equally wearied by his nights of watching and exposure, but his fears effectually banished sleep from his eyes. For three long hours, as we have said, he sat motionless on the dry-goods box, listening intently and wondering how his captivity was to end, and at the expiration of that time, he was frightened almost out of his senses by hearing a stealthy footfall outside the door of the wine-cellar, and the noise of a key grating in the lock. Utterly unable to speak, he sprang to his feet, and seizing his slumbering companion by the shoulders, shook him roughly.

"Ay! ay!" replied Wilson, drowsily. "I will be on deck in five minutes. Is Cuba in sight yet?"

"You are not on board the yacht," whispered Chase, recovering the use of his tongue by an effort, "but in the cellar of that old Creole's house; and here come the Spaniards to arrest us."

These words aroused Wilson, who rubbed his eyes and sat up on the dry-goods box just as the door opened, admitting a muffled figure in slouch hat and cloak, who carried a lighted lantern in his hand. Chase looked over the man's shoulder into the cellar beyond, expecting to see the troopers of whom he stood so much in fear; but their visitor was alone, and, if any faith was to be put in his actions, he had come there with anything but hostile intentions. He held his lantern aloft, and after gazing at the boys a moment, nodded his head and motioned to them to follow him. Wilson promptly obeyed, but Chase hung back.

"I am not sure that it will be safe," said he, doubtfully. "Perhaps we had better ask him to tell who sent him here, and what he intends to do with us."

"Let's follow him now and listen to his explanation afterward," replied Wilson. "I don't care much what he does with us, so long as he leads us into the open air. Anything is better than being shut up in this dark prison."

Chase was not fully satisfied on that point, but he was not allowed even a second to consider it. Wilson and their visitor moved off, and finding that he was about to be left alone in the dark, Chase stepped quickly out of the wine cellar and followed them. The man led the way to the stairs, which he ascended with noiseless footsteps, stopping now and then to listen, his every movement being imitated by the anxious captives. They reached the hall, and moved on tip-toe toward the door, which opened upon the back verandah; but just before they reached it their guide paused, and after giving each of the boys a warning gesture, raised his hand and stood pointing silently before him. The young sailors looked, and their hearts seemed to stop beating when they discovered, stretched out directly in front of the door, the burly form of one of the Spanish troopers. He slumbered heavily upon his blanket, one arm thrown over his head, and the other resting upon his carbine which lay across his breast. What was to be done now? was the question each of the boys asked himself, and which was quickly answered by their guide, who, with another warning gesture, moved forward, and stepping nimbly over the prostrated sentinel, beckoned to them to follow. Wilson at once responded and reached the verandah without arousing the sleeper; but it seemed as if Chase could not muster up courage enough to make the attempt.

"I can't do it," he whispered, in reply to Wilson's gestures of impatience. "Tell that man to come back and lead me out of the house by some other door."

"What good will it do to talk to him?" replied Wilson, in the same cautious whisper. "It is very evident from his actions that he can't talk English; and, besides, if there were any other way to get out, it isn't likely that he would have brought us here. I'd show a little pluck, if I were you. Come on."

"But what if that soldier should awake and spring up just as I was about to step over him?" continued Chase, in an ecstasy of alarm. "He'd catch me, sure."

"He will catch you if you stay there—you may depend upon that."

Chase might still have continued to argue the

point, had not the actions of the guide aroused him to a full sense of his situation. The man, who had been beckoning vehemently to him, suddenly faced about, and tapping Wilson on the shoulder, started down the steps that led from the verandah to the ground. Then Chase saw that he must follow or remain a prisoner in the house. He started and passed the sleeping sentinel in safety; but his mind was in such a whirl of excitement and terror that to save his life he could not have told how he did it. When he came to himself he and Wilson were following close at the heels of their guide, who was leading the way at a rapid run along the lane that led to the negro quarters.

"I wish I had never seen or heard of the Sportsman's Club," panted Chase, drawing his handkerchief across his forehead, for the exciting ordeal through which he had just passed, had brought the cold perspiration from every pore of his body; "I never was in a scrape like this before, and if I once get out of it you'll never see me in another. Fred Craven can take care of himself now; I am going home."

"When are you going to start?" asked Wilson.

"Just as soon as I reach the village."

"How are you going?"

"I don't know, and what's more, I don't care. I'll float there on a plank before I'll stay here twenty-four hours longer. There's another sentry. He's awake too, and coming toward us. Which way shall we run now?"

While Chase was speaking a man stepped into view from behind the fence and hurried toward them; but they soon found that there was no cause for alarm, for the new-comer was Don Casper himself.

"My lads," he exclaimed, gleefully, "I am overjoyed to see you once more, and in possession of your liberty too." And as he threw aside his cloak and extended a hand to each of them, the boys saw that he wore a sword by his side, and that his belt contained a brace of pistols. "This afternoon's work has ruined me," continued the Don, hurriedly. "It was very wrong in Captain Conway to send you out here in broad day-light, knowing as he does that I have long been suspected of being a rebel, and that the patrol were only waiting for some proof against me to arrest me. They've got that proof now, and my property will all be confiscated."

And now something happened which Wilson had feared and was on the lookout for—something which came very near placing him and his friend in a much worse predicament than they had yet got into. It was nothing more nor less than an effort on the part of Chase to explain matters to the Don. Wilson had thought over their situation since his release from the wine cellar, and he had come to the conclusion that, in the event of again meeting with their host, it would not be policy to attempt to correct the wrong impressions he had received concerning them, for the reason that it might prove a dangerous piece of business. He was afraid that the Don might not believe their story. In order to make him understand it, it would be necessary to go back to the day of the panther hunt, and describe what had then taken place between Bayard Bell and the members of the Sportsman's Club. That would consume a good deal of time, and there would be some things to tell that would look very unreasonable; and perhaps the Don would do as the captain of the revenue cutter had done—declare that it was all false. He would very likely think that the boys were trying to deceive him, and he might even go so far as to believe that they were in sympathy with the Spaniards, and that they had been employed by them to come to his house in the character of smugglers, on purpose to give the patrol an excuse for arresting him. This thought was enough to cause even the plucky Wilson some anxiety, and the longer he pondered upon it the more alarmed he became.

"We haven't seen the worst of it yet, I am afraid," he soliloquized. "We are in a much worse predicament than I thought. There will certainly be an explosion if the Don finds out that we are not the fellows he takes us for, and perhaps he'll be mad enough to smash things. He's got a good opinion of us now, and it would be foolish to say anything to change it. Our best plan will be to keep our mouths closed, and to get away from him without loss of time. If I only knew who wrote the note that negro gave him and what was in it, I would know just how to act."

Wilson waited for an opportunity to talk this plan over with Chase, but did not find it, for the reason that the Don made his appearance too quickly. The only course then left for him to pursue was to do all the talking himself, and allow his companion no chance to speak; but the latter was too smart for him, and with a dozen words brought about the very state of affairs that Wilson had hoped to guard against.

"You must not blame us for your misfortune," said Chase.

"I do not. It is Captain Conway's fault."

"He did not send us here—that is, we did not come by his orders. We are not smugglers, and neither have we any arms for you."

"Eh?" exclaimed the Don.

"We don't belong to the Stella, either. We came here in a private yacht, on our own private business, and know nothing about your transactions with Captain Conway."

"Gracias á Dios!" cried the Cuban; and the words came out from between his clenched teeth in a way that Chase did not like.

"Hold easy. Don't get angry until you hear my explanation. Remember that we have not tried to sail under false colors, since we have been here at your house. You did not ask us who we were, did' you? If you had given us the opportunity, we should have been glad to have appeared before you in our true characters, and to have explained the reason for our visit."

Having thus introduced his subject, Chase cleared his throat, thrust his hands into his pockets, and began a hurried and rather disconnected account of the events which had brought them to Cuba. The Don stood like a man in a dream. He was not listening to what the young sailor said, but was pondering upon some words he had uttered a few moments before. Suddenly he interrupted him.

"Your true character!" he exclaimed furiously. "Enough! That is all I wish to hear from you. I suspected you from the first. You have told me who you are *not*, and now I shall ascertain for myself who you *are*. The Stella is at the village, I know, for one of my negroes saw her there. I shall introduce you into the presence of Captain Conway before you are an hour older; and when he sees you, he will probably be able to tell me whether or not you came here by his orders. If he cannot vouch for you, you will find yourselves in serious trouble, I can tell you. I am now going to the stable after some horses, and you and your companion will move up into the shadow of this store-house and remain there, until I return, under the eye of my overseer, whom I shall instruct to shoot you down if you make the least attempt at escape."

Chase listened to this speech in utter amazement. His under jaw dropped down, and for a few seconds he stood gazing stupidly at the Don, who turned and began an earnest conversation in Spanish with his overseer—the man who had released the boys from the wine-cellar. At last he recovered himself in some measure, and made a bungling attempt to repair the damage he had done.

"I say, Don!" he exclaimed, "now you are laboring under another mistake, quite as bad as the first. You take us for Spanish sympathizers—I know you do, but we are not. We've got no interest in this fight, and we don't care which whips. I mean—you know—of course you Cubans are in the right, and we hope you will succeed in establishing your independence. I wish we had a whole cargo of arms for you, but we haven't. I wish the Banner was loaded so deep with them that she was on the point of sinking, but she isn't. O dear! I wish he would stop talking to that man and listen to me. I could set everything right in a few minutes. Speak to him, Wilson."

But his friend paid as little attention to him as the Don did. He stood narrowly watching the two men, and although he could not understand a word of their conversation, he knew pretty nearly what they were talking about. It was plain enough to him, too, that the overseer was as angry at them as his master was. He raised his lantern to allow its beams to fall full in their faces, scowled fiercely at each of them in turn, and then throwing aside his cloak and laying his hand on the butt of one of his pistols, motioned to them to follow him to the storehouse. As they obeyed the gesture, the Don hurried down the lane, not however without stopping long enough to tell the captives that the overseer was a good shot, and that an attempt to run away from him would be dangerous.

Never was a boy more astounded and alarmed than Chase was at that moment. Reaching the storehouse, he flung himself on the ground beside it in a state of utter dejection and misery. He looked at Wilson, who seated himself by his side, but even had there been light enough for him to see the expression that rested on the face of his friend, he would have found no encouragement there. Wilson was almost disheartened himself. Things looked even darker now than when they were confined in the wine-cellar—a state of affairs for which his companion was alone to blame. But Wilson had no fault to find. The mischief was done and could not be undone; and like a sensible fellow, he determined to make the best of it, and say nothing about it.

"Don't I wish I had never seen or heard of the Sportsman's Club!" said Chase, feebly. "I wonder if that overseer understands English? Try him, Wilson. I want to say something to you."

Wilson, for want of something better to do, addressed a few words to their guard, who stood close at their side, keeping a sharp eye on their movements, but he only shook his head, and threw aside his cloak to show his pistols.

"I think you may speak freely," said Wilson. "What were you going to say?"

"We're in trouble again," replied Chase.

"O! Is that all? It's no news."

"I wish I had not tried to explain matters."

"So do I."

"Is there nothing we can do? Let's jump up and take to our heels. I'll risk the bullets in the overseer's pistols, if you will."

"What's the use? Where shall we run to?"

"To town, of course We want to go back to the yacht, don't we?"

"Certainly. But if we wait a few minutes, the Don will bring us some horses, and then we can ride there. That will be much easier than walking, and safer too; for not knowing the way, we might get lost in the darkness, or run against some of the patrols on the road."

"Do you intend to go to town with the Don?" asked Chase, in great amazement.

"I do."

"Well, if you don't beat all the fellows I ever heard of! You have certainly taken leave of your senses. Don't you know that Captain Conway and Mr. Bell will do all they can to strengthen the Don's suspicions?"

"You didn't hear me through. We don't want to see either of those worthy gentlemen, if we can avoid it. We will go with the Don, simply because we can't help ourselves, and perhaps during the ride he will get over his mad fit, so that we can talk to him. If he does, we will tell him our story from beginning to end, and ask him to go aboard the Banner with us. Walter and the other fellows must have returned by this time, and when the Don finds that their story agrees with ours, and sees the yacht's papers, perhaps he will believe us. If he don't, let's see him help himself. We'll be on board our vessel then, and we'll stay there."

"Yes. That's all very nice. But suppose the Banner isn't there? What then?"

"Eh?" exclaimed Wilson.

"Those deserters may have returned and run off with her during our absence. What would you do in that case?"

"I don't know. I wasn't calculating on that."

"And what will the Don do?" continued Chase. "If we tell him that we shall find our yacht at the wharf and she happens to be gone, he will have more reason to suspect us than he does now."

Wilson looked at his companion, and then settling back against the storehouse, went off into a brown study; while Chase, after waiting a few minutes for him to say something, sprang to his feet, and began pacing nervously back and forth. Just then, an incident happened which created a diversion in favor of the two boys, and which they were prompt to take advantage of, only in different ways.

CHAPTER IX.

WILSON RUNS A RACE.

THE diversion of which we have spoken was caused by the sound of stealthy footsteps, and an indistinct murmur of voices which came from the opposite side of the storehouse. Somebody was coming down the lane. Believing that it was the Don returning with the horses, Wilson arose slowly to his feet and stood awaiting the orders of the guard, while Chase stopped his walk and looked first one way and then the other, as if he were going to run off as soon as he could make up his mind which direction to take. The actions of the overseer, however, seemed to indicate that there was some one besides the Don approaching—some one whom he had not been expecting and whom he did not care to see. He stood for a few seconds listening to the footsteps and voices, and then moving quickly into the shadow of the storehouse, crouched close to the ground, muttering Spanish ejaculations and acting altogether as if he were greatly perplexed. His behavior did not escape the notice of Wilson, and it at once suggested to him the idea of escape. His first impulse was to rush out of his concealment and throw himself upon the protection of the new-comers; but sober second thought stepped in and told him that it would be a good plan to first ascertain who they were. He moved to the corner of the storehouse, and looking up the lane, saw four men approaching. They were dressed like sailors—he could see their wide trowsers and jaunty hats, dark as it was—and he noticed that two of them carried handspikes on their shoulders. They were so near to him that he was afraid to move lest he should attract their attention, and they came still nearer to him with every step they took. They were directing their course toward the storehouse, talking earnestly as they approached, and presently some startling words, uttered by a familiar voice, fell upon his ear.

"I tell you this is the house. I guess I know what I am about. When I first discovered it the negroes belonging to the plantation were gathered here in a crowd, and a white man was serving them with corn-meal and bacon. All we've got to do is to bust open this door, and we'll find provisions enough to last us on a cruise around the world. Now, Bob, I want you to clap a stopper on that jaw of yours and hush your growling. If I don't take you safely to Havana, I'll agree to sign over to you all the prize money I win in that privateer."

"I ain't growling about that," replied another familiar voice. "I don't like the idea of stealing private yachts and running away with them. It looks too much like piracy."

"Well, it can't be helped now. The Banner is ours, and the best thing we can do is to use her while we've got her. Give me that handspike and I'll soon open this door. Keep your weather eyes open, the rest of you."

Wilson listened as if fascinated; and when the conversation ceased, and the door began to creak and groan as the handspike was brought to bear upon it, he thrust his head farther around the corner of the storehouse, and at the imminent risk of being seen by the men, who were scarcely more than four feet distant, took a good survey of the group. His ears had not deceived him. The men who had thus unexpectedly intruded their presence upon him, were none other than Tomlinson and the rest of the deserters from the revenue cutter. He could distinctly see every one of them. Tomlinson was engaged in breaking open the door of the storehouse, and the others stood a little farther off, some looking up and the rest down the lane.

"Now here's a go," thought Wilson, so excited that he scarcely knew what he was about. "Them fellows have stolen the Banner, and are preparing to supply themselves with provisions for their voyage to Havana. What will become of us if we don't get that boat back again? They shan't have her. We'll slip away from this overseer and turn their triumph into defeat before they are ten minutes older."

Wilson turned to look at the guard. The man was standing close behind him, and seemed to be awaiting the result of his investigations. Acting upon a resolution he had suddenly formed, the young sailor stepped aside, and motioned to him to look around the corner of the building. The man complied, and no sooner was his back turned, than Wilson ran swiftly, but noiselessly, along the side of the storehouse, looking everywhere for Chase; but the latter was not in sight Greatly surprised at his sudden disappearance, and almost ready to doubt the evidence of his eyes, he glanced along the building again and again, and even spoke his friend's name as loudly as he dared, but without receiving any response.

"He has watched his chance and taken himself off," thought Wilson. "I'll soon find him, and if we don't upset the plans of Tomlinson and his crew, I shall miss my guess. Good-by, Mr. Overseer! When the Don returns and asks where your prisoners are, you may tell him you don't know."

So saying, Wilson dodged around the corner of the storehouse, and struck off toward the beach with all the speed he could command.

And where was Chase all this time? If Wilson had known the reason for his disappearance, he would not have had a very high opinion of his friend. That worthy had been thinking deeply since his last conversation with Wilson, and had at length hit upon what he conceived to be a remarkably brilliant plan for extricating himself from his troubles.

"The expedition is a failure—that's plain enough to be seen," he had said to himself; "and instead of trying to rescue Fred Craven, it strikes me that it would be a good plan to look out for our own safety. I am not going back to town with the Don, and the only way to avoid it is to desert. Yes, sir, that's just what I'll do. I shall be much safer alone than in the company of such fellows as this Wilson and Walter Gaylord, who are continually getting themselves and others into trouble, and I'll see home before they do, I'll warrant. I'll get out of Cuba, at any rate. I'll ship aboard the first vessel that leaves port, I don't care if she takes me to South America."

It never occurred to Chase, while he was congratulating himself upon this idea, that, in carrying it into execution, he would be making a very poor return for Wilson's kindness and friendship. He forgot the fidelity with which the latter had clung to him through thick and thin, and the assistance he had rendered him in inducing Walter Gaylord to interest himself in his affairs. All he thought of was his own safety. The approach of the deserters was a most fortunate thing for him, for it gave him the very opportunity he was waiting for. He heard the voices and the footsteps, and the alarm the sounds at first produced gave way to a feeling of exultation, when he saw Wilson and the overseer move cautiously toward the opposite end of the storehouse. Had he waited a minute longer he might have escaped in company with his friend, and saved himself a good many exciting adventures which we have yet to relate; but the guard with his dreaded pistols was at the farther end of the building, and the chance was too good to be lost. He sprang around the corner of the storehouse, and in an instant was out of sight in the darkness.

Wilson, little dreaming what had become of him, pursued his way with rapid footsteps across the field toward the beach, taking care to keep the negro quarters between him and the men at the storehouse. He kept his eyes roving through the darkness in every direction, in the hope of discovering Chase, but was disappointed.

"He can't be far away, and when I come up with him, I will tell him how we can beat these deserters at their own game," chuckled the young sailor, highly elated over the plans he had formed. "If they came here in the Banner, she must be at anchor somewhere along the beach. As there are but four of them, and they are all at the storehouse, it follows as a thing of course that they must have left the yacht unguarded. It will be the easiest thing in the world to swim off to her, hoist the sails, and put to sea before they know what is going on. I declare, there's Chase now, and the yacht, too! Hurrah!"

Wilson had by this time arrived within sight of the little bay, which set into the shore at this place, and just then, the rays of the moon, struggling through a rift in the clouds, gave him a fair view of the scene before him. The first object his eyes rested upon was the yacht, riding at anchor about a quarter of a mile from the shore. The next, was a stone jetty extending out into the water, beside which were moored several boats. In one of them a sail was hoisted. This was probably the one which the deserters intended to use to convey the stolen provisions on board the yacht. The third object was a human figure, standing on the beach near the jetty. He wore a cloak and a slouch hat, and Wilson thought he recognised in him his missing friend, although he at the same time wondered how he had come by the articles named, for he certainly had not worn them the last time he saw him. Hearing the sound of his approach, the figure stepped upon the jetty and moved nervously about, as if undecided whether to take to his heels or wait until he came up.

"Don't be alarmed, Chase; it is I," exclaimed Wilson, as soon as he came within speaking distance. "What possessed you to run off without saying a word to me? It is only by good luck that I have found you again. Do you see what those deserters have been doing?" he added, pointing to the yacht. "Let's get into one of these boats and take possession of her before they return. We've got the best right to her."

Wilson, who had shouted out these words as he approached the figure, was a good deal surprised at the manner in which his proposition was received. It did not meet with the ready response he had expected, for the figure, whoever he was, remained perfectly motionless and said nothing. That was not at all like Chase, and Wilson began to believe there was something wrong somewhere. He stopped a few feet from the figure, and peering sharply at him, discovered, to his great surprise, that the slouch hat covered a face that did not at all resemble his friend's. It was a bearded face—an evil face—a face that was quite familiar to him, and which he had hoped never to see again.

"Pierre!" he exclaimed, in alarm.

"'Tain't nobody else," was the reply.

For the next few seconds, the two stood looking at one another without speaking—Wilson wondering what was to be done now, and trying in vain to find some explanation for the smuggler's presence there, and the latter evidently enjoying the boy's bewilderment.

"What are you doing on this plantation?" asked the young sailor, breaking the silence at last.

"I might ask you the same question, I reckon. We thought you were captured by the Spaniards long ago. That's what we sent you out here for."

"*We?* Who are we?"

"Mr. Bell, Captain Conway, and the rest of us."

"Ah!" exclaimed Wilson, so indignant at this avowal that he forgot all his fear; "then Chase and I were right in our surmises. Well, your little plans didn't work, did they? But you have not yet told me what you are doing here. How came you in company with these deserters; and how did you get possession of the yacht?"

"That's Mr. Bell's business."

"So, he had something to do with it, had he? I thought as much. Where are Walter and the rest of the fellows?"

"We left them somewhere about the village."

"Where have you started for—Havana?"

"That's another thing that don't interest you."

"Yes, it does. I know you are going there, and that you will start as soon as Tomlinson comes back with the provisions. Will you take me with you?"

"Not much. We've got all the crew we want."

"Why, Pierre!" exclaimed Wilson, "you surely do not mean to leave me here? I am all alone. Chase has left me, and I haven't seen Walter and the rest of the fellows since four o'clock this afternoon."

"Well, I can't help that, can I?"

"How am I to get home, if you go away in the Banner?"

"That's your lookout."

"Now, what have I done to you, that you should treat me in this way?"

"You have been meddling with our business—that's what you have done," answered Pierre, fiercely. "You ought to have stayed in Bellville, while you were there, and attended to your own concerns. We don't care whether or not you ever get back."

Wilson, with an air of utter dejection, seated himself on the jetty, while Pierre, who took a savage delight in tormenting the boy, thrust his hands into his pockets and began pacing back and forth on the beach. The crew of the yacht had caused the smugglers considerable anxiety, and they had shown so much courage and perseverance in their pursuit of the Stella, that they had raised the ire of every one of her company, and Pierre was glad of this opportunity to obtain some slight satisfaction; but had he known all that was passing in the boy's mind, he would have found that he had even more spirit and determination to deal with than he imagined. Wilson was only playing a part. He was firm in his resolution to recover the yacht, but knowing that he could not cope with Pierre openly, he resorted to strategy. By pretending to be completely cowed by the smuggler's fierce words and manner, he had thrown the latter off his guard; and when he walked past him and took his seat on the jetty, Pierre did not raise any objections. By this manœuvre, Wilson gained a position between the man and the nearest boat, which happened to be the one with the sail hoisted. That was the first step accomplished. The next was to draw Pierre's attention to something, if it were only for a moment, until he could run to the boat, cast off the painter, and fill away for the yacht. He was not long in hitting upon a plan.

"I know what I shall do," said he, at length. "I'll stay here until Tomlinson comes, and ask him if he won't take me aboard the Banner."

"I can tell you now that he won't do it," replied Pierre.

"I don't care; I'll ask him, any way. If I can only go to Havana, that's all I want. I shall be able to find some vessel there bound for the States. He's coming now."

Pierre paused in his walk and looked toward the plantation house, but could see nothing. He listened, but all he heard was the roar of the surf on the beach.

"I can hear them," continued Wilson, rising to his feet; "and they're in trouble too. They're running and shouting. There! did you hear that gun?"

Pierre listened again, and then walked a few steps up the beach to get a little farther away from the surf. A moment later he heard the sound of rapid footfalls, and turned quickly to see Wilson flying along the jetty toward the boat.

"Stop!" he roared, springing forward in pursuit

The Race for the Yacht.

the instant he divined the boy's intention. "You are not going aboard that yacht."

"That depends upon whether I do or not," shouted Wilson, in reply.

The race that followed was short but highly exciting. Wilson sped along as swiftly as a bird on the wing, scarcely seeming to touch the ground; while the clumsy Pierre puffed and blowed like a high pressure steamboat; and finding that he was encumbered by his heavy cloak, threw it aside, and even discarded his hat; but all to no purpose. Wilson made such good use of his time that he succeeded in reaching the boat and jumping into it, before his pursuer came up; but there his good fortune seemed to end. He could not cast off the painter. One end of it was passed around one of the thwarts, and the other made fast to a ring in the jetty, and both knots were jammed so that he could not undo them. He pulled, and tugged, and panted in vain. He felt for his knife to cut the rope, but could not find it. As a last resort he seized the thwart with both hands, and exerting all his strength, wrenched it loose from its fastenings, and threw it overboard, at the same time placing his shoulder against the jetty, and with a strong push, sending the boat from the shore. With a cry of triumph he seized the sheet which was flapping in the wind, passed it around a cleat with one hand and seized the tiller with the other. The boat began to gather headway, but just a moment too late. Pierre, all out of breath, and full of rage, now came up, and seeing that the boy was about to escape him, threw himself, without an instant's hesitation, headlong into the water. He fell just astern of the boat, and although Wilson hauled hard on the sheet, and crowded her until she stood almost on her side, he could not make her go fast enough to get out of the man's reach. He made a blind clutch as he arose to the surface, and fastened with a firm grip upon the rudder.

"Now, then!" exclaimed Pierre, fiercely, "I reckon you'll stop, won't you?"

Wilson was frightened, but he did not lose his presence of mind. Had he spent even a second in considering what ought to be done, his capture would have been certain, for the smuggler clung to the rudder with one hand, and stretched out the other to seize the stern of the boat.

"Pierre," said the boy, "if you want that piece of wood, you may have it. I can get along without it.' And with a quick movement he unshipped the rudder, and the boat flew on, leaving it in the man's grasp.

The little craft, now being without a steering apparatus, quickly fell off and lost headway, and Pierre, with a loud yell of rage, threw away the rudder and struck out vigorously, expecting to overtake her; but Wilson seized the sheet in his teeth, picked up one of the oars that lay under the thwarts, dropped the blade into the water, and in less time than it takes to tell it, the boat was again under control, and rapidly leaving Pierre behind.

"There, sir!" said Wilson; "I did it, but I wouldn't go through the same thing again to be made an admiral. I've got the yacht in my undisputed possession, or shall have in a few minutes, and what shall I do with her? Shall I lay off and on and make signals for Chase, or shall I go back to the village after Walter and the other fellows? Come on, old boy! I am well out of your reach."

This last remark was addressed to Pierre, who, having been washed ashore by the surf, had run to one of the boats that were moored to the jetty, and was hoisting a sail, preparatory to pursuing Wilson. This movement caused the young sailor no uneasiness. He had a long start, and he knew that he could reach the yacht, slip the anchor, and get under way before Pierre could come up. He kept one eye on the man, and pondered upon the questions he had just asked himself; but before he had come to any decision, he found himself alongside the yacht. As he rounded to under her bow, he thought he heard a slight movement on her deck. He listened intently, but the sound was not repeated; and after a little hesitation, he placed his hands upon the rail, drew himself up and looked over. He saw no one, but he soon found that that was no proof there was no one there, for, as he sprang upon the yacht's deck, and ran forward to slip the anchor, his feet were suddenly pulled from under him, and he fell forward on his face. Before he could move or cry out, some one threw himself across his shoulders, and seizing both his hands, pinned them to the deck.

CHAPTER X.

A LUCKY FALL.

"ARE we not in luck for once in our lives? Who would have thought that the storm which blew us so far out of our course, was destined to prove an advantage instead of a hindrance to us?"

"Not I, for one, but I can see it now. If we had gone to Havana, as we intended, we should never have seen the Stella again, or Featherweight either. Now that we have found him, what is the next thing to be done?"

"We'll talk about that as we go along, and keep them in sight until we have decided upon a plan of action. There they go over the hill. Let's hurry on, for we must allow them no chance to give us the slip."

This conversation was carried on by Walter and Perk, as they ran up the hill in pursuit of Fred Craven, whom they had seen going toward the village in company with Mr. Bell and Captain Conway. They knew it was Fred, and they knew too that he saw them, and was aware that they were following him, for once, just before he disappeared from their sight, he drew his handkerchief from his pocket and waved it in the air behind him. The movement was executed with but little attempt at concealment; but, although the Captain and Mr. Bell must certainly have seen it, they made no effort to check it.

As we have seen, from the few words that passed between them, the young sailors had left the yacht without any very definite object in view. They wanted to assist Fred Craven, if the opportunity were presented, but just how they were going to set about it they could not tell. Should they hurry on, and when they came up with him demand his release; or should they wait and see what his captors were going to do with him? While they were talking the matter over, the objects of their pursuit disappeared over the brow of the hill, and that was the last they saw of them, although they at once quickened their pace to a run, and in a few seconds were standing on the very spot where they had last seen them. They looked in every direction, but the men and their captive had vanished. Before them was a wide and level road, leading through the village and into the plain beyond, and they could see every moving thing in it for the distance of a mile. There were people there in abundance, but none among them who looked like Fred Craven and his keepers. Where could they have gone so suddenly?

"Now this beats everything I ever heard of," said Walter in great bewilderment. "We are not dreaming, are we?"

"No sir," replied Perk, emphatically. "I was never more fully awake than I am at this moment. There's some trick at the bottom of this."

"What in the world is it?"

"I should be glad to tell you if I knew. You take one side of the street, and I'll take the other. Don't waste time now, but be careful to look into every shop and behind every house you pass."

Walter, prompt to act upon the suggestion, set off at the top of his speed, followed by Perk, who, although equally anxious to get over a good deal of ground in the shortest possible space of time, conducted his search with more care. Had the former looked into one of the cross-streets past which he hurried with such frantic haste, he might, perhaps, have caught a partial glimpse of the burly form of

Captain Conway standing in a doorway; and had he approached him he would have found Mr. Bell and Featherweight standing close behind him. But he did not know this, and neither was he aware that as soon as he and Perk passed on down the street, the master of the smuggling vessel came cautiously from his place of concealment, and looking around the corner of a house, watched them until they were two hundred yards away. But the Captain did this, and more. Having satisfied himself that the young tars had been eluded, he returned to the doorway and held a short conversation with Mr. Bell. When it was ended, that gentleman hurried off out of sight, and the Captain, drawing Fred's arm through his own, conducted him along the cross-street and through lanes and by-ways back to the wharf, and on board a vessel—not the Stella, but a large ship, which, if one might judge by the bustle and confusion on her deck, was just on the point of sailing. As he and his captive boarded her, they were met by the master of the vessel who, without saying a word, led them into his cabin and showed them an open state-room. Without any ceremony Fred was pushed into it, the door closed and the key turned in the lock.

"There," said Captain Conway, with a sigh of relief, "he is disposed of at last. If any of those Banner fellows can find him now, I should like to see them do it. Mr. Bell's been in this business too long to be beaten by a lot of little boys."

This was only a part of Mr. Bell's plan; and while it was being carried into execution, some other events, a portion of which we have already described, were taking place in the harbor. The mate of the smuggling vessel visited the yacht, and after enticing Tomlinson and the rest of the deserters on board the Stella by the promise of a good breakfast, and a pipe to smoke after it, and starting off Wilson and his companion on a wild-goose chase, by sending them a note purporting to come from Walter, had cleared the coast so that he could carry out the rest of his employer's scheme without let or hindrance. The first thing he did was to convey some bales and boxes containing arms, ammunition and military trappings, on board the yacht—for what purpose we shall see presently—and his second to secure possession of Walter's clearance papers. When these things had been done, the mate returned on board the Stella and received some more instructions from Mr. Bell; after which he came out of the cabin and joined the deserters who were in the forecastle, discussing the breakfast that had been prepared for them. By adroit questioning he finally obliged Tomlinson to confess what he had all along suspected—that he and his companions belonged to the United States revenue service, and that they had deserted their vessel and stolen a passage across the Gulf, with the intention of shipping aboard a Cuban privateer. When the mate had found out all he wanted to know, he left them with the remark that there was a privateer lying off Havana, all ready to sail as soon as she had shipped a crew, and that if the deserters wanted to find her they had better start at once. He added that they might waste a good deal of valuable time if they waited for a vessel to take them to the city, and that the best thing for them to do would be to steal a small sail-boat. There were plenty of them about the harbor. Havana was only a hundred miles away, and with a fair wind they could sail there in a few hours. If they adopted that plan, they had better wait until dark in order to escape the vigilance of the Spanish officials, who boarded all vessels, even skiffs, as they entered and left the port.

"What have you fellows got to say to that?"

asked Tomlinson, as soon as the officer had ascended to the deck. "The mate's plan agrees with mine exactly, and that proves that it is worth trying. We will go back and take the Banner as soon as we have finished our breakfast. I am going, at least, and I'd like to know who is with me. Speak up!"

All the deserters spoke up except Bob. He grumbled as usual, and had some objections to offer. "Tom," said he, "you haven't yet answered the question I asked you once before: who's going to navigate the vessel? You can't do it."

"Can't I? What's the reason? All we've got to do is to follow the coast."

"And get lost or wrecked for our pains! No, thankee. And there's another thing you haven't thought of. We shall want some clearance papers, and how are we going to get 'em? That officer who boarded us as we came in will be sure to visit us again. The mate said so."

"We're going to give him the slip."

"But suppose we can't do it? What if he sees us and hails us?"

"We won't stop, that's all. He goes around in a row-boat, and the yacht will easily run away from her."

"You forget that there are two men of war in the harbor, and a fort on the point. I don't care to run the fire of a hundred guns in such a craft as the Banner. Put me on board the old gunboat Cairo, if she was as good as before she was sunk by that rebel torpedo in Yazoo river, and I wouldn't mind it."

"We're not going to run the fire of a hundred guns, or one either," replied Tomlinson. "I'll tell you just how we will manage it. "We'll take the Banner at once; that's the first thing to be done. Then we'll run her over to the other side of the harbor—there are no wharves there, you know—and anchor off shore until dark, when we will make sail and slip out; and no one will be the wiser for it."

"But we shall want something to eat," persisted Bob. "There isn't a mouthful on board the yacht. We may meet with head winds, you know, and be a week reaching Havana."

"Haven't I told you that it will be the easiest thing in the world to land somewhere on the coast and steal some grub?" demanded Tomlinson, losing all patience.

"So it will, mate, and I know just where to get

it," said a strange voice, in a suppressed whisper above their heads.

The deserters, not a little alarmed to find that their conversation had been overheard, glanced quickly upward and saw a man crouching at the top of the ladder and looking down at them. It was Pierre, who having thus addressed them, made a gesture of silence, and after looking all around the deck as if fearful of being seen, crept down the ladder into the forecastle.

"Don't be alarmed, lads," he continued, in a hurried whisper. "I heard what you said, because I couldn't well help it, being at work close by the hatchway, and you talked louder than you thought, I reckon. If you will let me, I will strike hands with you. I have been watching all day for a chance to desert this craft, for I want to join that privateer myself. If I can do that, I shall be a rich man in less than six months. I like your plans, and will help you carry them out. Now is the best time in the world to capture that yacht, for there is nobody on board of her. I know just where to find the privateer, and, while we are on the way, I will show you where we can get all the grub we want."

Pierre rattled off this speech as if he had learned it by heart—as indeed he had, his teacher being none other than Mr. Bell—and spoke so rapidly that his auditors could not have crowded a word in edgewise if they had tried. When he finished, he seated himself on one of the berths and looked inquiringly from one to the other, waiting for their answer. It was not given at once, for Bob and his two companions were not disposed to advance an opinion until they had heard what their leader had to say; and the latter, surprised and disconcerted by Pierre's sudden appearance and his unexpected offer of assistance, wanted time to collect his wits and propound a few inquiries. He wanted to know who Pierre was; how long he had been on board the Stella; if he was certain there was a privateer lying off Havana waiting for a crew; how he had found out that she was there, and all that. The smuggler gave satisfactory replies to these questions, and then Tomlinson extended his hand, and told him that he was glad to see him. Their new acquaintance, being thus admitted into their confidence, helped himself to a piece of hard-tack, and during the conversation that followed succeeded in convincing the deserters that he was just the man they wanted; he knew how things ought to be managed in order to insure complete success. So certain was Tomlinson of this fact that, with the consent of his companions, he offered Pierre the command of the party, and agreed to be governed by his orders.

"Well, then," said Pierre, "it is all settled, and the sooner we are on the move the better. If you have finished your breakfast, go out on the wharf and wait for me. I will be on hand as soon as I can find a chance to leave the vessel without being seen."

The deserters accordingly left the forecastle, and as soon as they were out of sight Pierre followed them to the deck and entered the cabin, where he found Mr. Bell. After a few minutes' interview with that gentleman, he came out again, holding in his hands a roll of bills, which he showed to the mate whom he met at the top of the companion ladder. He was now about to carry out the rest of Mr. Bell's plan, and the money he carried in his hand was the reward for his services.

In order to keep up appearances, and make the deserters, who were watching him from the wharf, believe that he was really leaving the vessel without the knowledge of her crew, Pierre, after gathering up some of his clothes, walked carelessly about the deck until the mate's back was turned, and then vaulting over the rail, ran quickly behind a pile of cotton bales on the wharf; and having joined Tomlinson and the rest, led the way to the place where the Banner lay. They boarded the little vessel as if they had a perfect right to be there, and without any delay began hoisting the sails. While thus engaged Tomlinson happened to look up the harbor, and to his great disgust discovered Eugene and Bab hurrying along the wharf.

"What's to be done now, captain?" he asked, directing Pierre's attention to the two boys. "There come some of them young sea-monkeys, and we can't get under way before they board us. They're always around when they are not wanted."

Pierre's actions, upon hearing these words, not a little surprised Tomlinson. He took just one glance at the young sailors, and then springing to the fore-hatch, lowered himself quickly into the galley. There he stopped long enough to give a few brief and hurried orders to the deserters, one of whom also jumped down into the galley, while the others went on with the work of hoisting the sails. A few minutes later, Eugene and Bab crossed the deck of the brig that lay between the yacht and the wharf, and appeared at the rail.

"What's going on here?" demanded the former, angrily. "It seems to me, Tomlinson, that you are taking a good many liberties on so short an acquaintance. I was in hopes I had seen the last of you. Drop those halliards."

"Of course I will, if you say so, because you are one of the owners of the yacht," replied the sailor. "But we have orders from the lieutenant to get under way at once."

"From Chase?"

"Yes, sir."

"Where is he?" asked Bab.

"He's below, and Wilson has gone out to look for you."

"Has Walter returned yet?"

"Yes. He is in the cabin now."

"Why is he getting under way, and where is he starting for?" inquired Eugene, as he and Bab swung themselves over the brig's rail and dropped upon the deck of their vessel.

"I don't exactly know. There's been something

exciting going on here. He will tell you all about it."

"Did Walter bring any one with him when he came back?"

"Yes; another boy."

"What's his name—Fred Craven?" demanded Bab and Eugene, in a breath.

"I don't know. Never saw or heard of him before. He's a little fellow—about as big as a marline-spike."

"That's Featherweight!" cried Eugene.

"I know it is," shouted Bab. "Hurrah for our side."

Without waiting to ask any more questions, the two boys bounded toward the door of the cabin, each one striving to outrun the other, and to be the first to greet the long-lost secretary. Bab took the lead, and a fortunate thing it was for Eugene. The latter, in his haste, caught his foot in one of the foresail halliards, and was sent headlong to the deck, while Bab kept on, and jumping into the standing room, pushed open the door of the cabin; but he did not enter. He stopped short on the threshold and stood there motionless, until a brawny hand fastened upon the collar of his jacket and jerked him through the door.

Eugene quickly recovered his feet, and arrived within sight of the entrance to the cabin just an instant after Bab disappeared. He too paused, amazed at what he saw. The first thing he noticed, was that the lock had been forced from the door (Chase had locked it before leaving the yacht, and Pierre had used a handspike to open it), and that would have aroused a suspicion of treachery in his mind, even had he not seen Bab struggling in the grasp of two men, both of whom he recognised. One was Bob, and the other was Pierre. Eugene stooped down and looked into the cabin, and seeing that there was no one there except the two ruffians and their prisoner, comprehended the situation almost as well as if it had been explained to him. He could not of course, tell how Pierre came to be there in company with the deserters, but he knew that they were about to steal the yacht, and that Tomlinson had concocted the story he had told in order to send him and Bab into the cabin, so that they could be secured. Poor Bab had been' entrapped, and the only thing that saved Eugene, was the accident that had befallen him.

"Pierre," shouted the boy, in indignant tones, "I know what you're at, but your plan won't work. You'll not get far away with the Banner—mind that!"

Pierre at once left his companion to attend to Bab, and came out into the standing room, eager to secure Eugene, before his loud, angry voice attracted the attention of the brig's crew. "You will save yourself trouble by clapping a stopper on that jaw of yours," said he, fiercely. "Come up behind him, Tomlinson, and the rest of you cast off the lines, and get the Banner under way without the loss of a moment."

"The rest of you let those lines alone," shouted Eugene. "And Tomlinson, you keep your distance," he added, springing lightly upon the taffrail as the deserter advanced upon him. "You'll not take me into that cabin a prisoner."

"Grab him, Tomlinson!" exclaimed Pierre, "and be quick about it, or you'll be too late."

And he *was* too late, being altogether too slow in his movements to seize so agile a fellow as Eugene. Believing that the boy was fairly cornered and could not escape, the deserter came up very deliberately, and was much surprised to see him raise his hands above his head, and dive out of sight in the harbor. Tomlinson ran quickly to the stern and looked over, but Eugene was far out of his reach, being just in the act of disappearing around the stern of the brig.

"Never mind him," said Pierre; "he's gone, and we can't help it. The next thing is to be gone ourselves, before he gets help and comes back."

"All clear fore and aft!" cried one of the deserters.

"Shove off, for'ard!" commanded Pierre, seizing the wheel. "Tom, send two men aloft to shake out those topsails."

In five minutes more the Banner, lying almost on her side, and carrying a huge bone in her teeth, was scudding swiftly away from the wharf toward the opposite side of the harbor.

CHAPTER XI.

"SHEEP AHOY!"

MEANWHILE Eugene, whose astonishment and indignation knew no bounds, was striking out vigorously for the wharf. Like Chase he began to believe he had ample reason for declaring the expedition a failure, and to wish he had known better than to urge it on. The yacht was lost, with no prospect of being recovered; Bab was a prisoner in the hands of the deserters, and there was no knowing what they would do with him; he was alone, in a strange country, his brother and all the rest of the Club having disappeared; and Fred Craven was still missing—perhaps had already been sent off to Mexico under the Spanish sea captain. This was the worst feature in the case, and it caused Eugene more anxiety than the loss of the yacht. Concerning himself he was not at all uneasy. He was in full possession of his liberty, was a passable sailor, and could easily find a vessel bound for the States;

but what could poor Fred do in his helpless condition? Eugene was so fully occupied with such thoughts as these that he forgot that he was in the water; and neither did he know that he was an object of interest and amusement to several men who were watching him. But he became aware of the fact when he rounded the brig's stern, for a voice directly over his head called out, in a strong foreign accent:

"Sheep ahoy!"

"You're a sheep yourself," replied Eugene, looking up, just in time to catch a line as it came whirling down to him, and to see half a dozen sailors in striped shirts and tarpaulins, leaning over the brig's rail. Seizing the line with both hands he was drawn out of the water, and in a few seconds more found himself sprawling on the vessel's deck in the midst of the sailors, who greeted him with jeers and shouts of laughter.

"Now, perhaps you see something funny in this, but I don't," exclaimed Eugene, as he scrambled to his feet and looked around for the Banner. "Do you see that craft out there? She belongs to my brother, and those fellows have stolen her and are running away with her. I am a stranger to this country, and its laws and ways of doing business, and I don't know how to go to work to get her back. Perhaps some of you will be kind enough to give me a word of advice."

The sailors ceased their laughter when he began to speak, and listened attentively until he was done, when they broke out into another roar, louder than the first. The one who had thrown him the rope slapped him on the back and shouted "Sheep ahoy!" while another offered him a plug of tobacco. The truth was, they had seen Eugene jump overboard when Tomlinson came aft to seize him; and, very far from guessing the facts of the case, they believed him to be one of the yacht's boys who had taken to the water to escape punishment for some offence he had committed. They could not understand English, and there was only one among them who could speak even a word of it; and all he could say was "Sheep ahoy!" (he intended it for "Ship ahoy!") which he kept repeating over and over again, without having the least idea what it meant. They thought that Eugene was trying to explain to them how badly he had been abused on board his vessel, and his vehement gestures and angry countenance excited their mirth.

"Get away with that stuff!" cried the boy, hitting the plug of tobacco a knock that sent it from the sailor's hand spinning across the deck. "Stop pounding me on the back, you fellow, and shouting 'Sheep ahoy!' I'm no more of a sheep than you are. Is there one among you who can talk English?"

"Sheep ahoy!" yelled the sailor, while his companions burst into another roar of laughter, as the owner of the tobacco went to pick up his property.

The harder Eugene tried to make himself understood, the louder the sailors laughed. At first he thought they would not answer his questions, merely because they wished to tantalize him; but being satisfied at last that they could not comprehend a word he said, he pushed them roughly aside, and springing upon the wharf, hurried off, followed by a fresh burst of laughter and loud cries of " Sheep ahoy!"

"I don't see any sense in making game of a fellow that way, even if you can't understand him," thought Eugene, more angry than ever. "I hope the rebels may capture the last one of you, and shut you up for awhile."

Eugene did not know where he was going or

what he intended to do. Indeed, he did not give the matter a moment's thought. All he cared for just then was to get out of hearing of the laughter of the brig's crew, and to find some quiet spot where he could sit down by himself, and take time to recover from the bewilderment occasioned by the events of the last quarter of an hour. With this object in view, he hurried along the wharf, out of the gate, and up the street leading to the top of the hill. At the same moment Walter and Perk were walking slowly up the other side. It was now nearly sunset. For four long hours the young captain and his companion had run about the village in every direction, looking for Fred Craven, and now, almost tired out, and utterly discouraged, they were slowly retracing their steps toward the wharf. They met Eugene at the top of the hill, and the moment their eyes rested on him, they knew he had some unwelcome news to communicate, although they little thought it as bad as it was.

"O, fellows!" exclaimed Eugene, as soon as he came within speaking distance, "you don't know how glad I am to see you again. They've got her at last, and Bab too; and here the rest of us are, high and dry ashore, with a fair prospect of working our passage back to Bellville, if we can find any vessel to ship on. Look there!"

Walter turned his eyes in the direction indicated, and one look was enough. "The deserters?" he faltered.

"Yes, sir, the deserters! And who do you suppose is their leader? Pierre Coulte!"

Without waiting to hear the exclamations of amazement which this unexpected intelligence called forth from his companions, Eugene went on to tell what had happened to him since he had last seen his brother—how he and Bab had traversed the wharf from one end to the other without meeting the revenue officer of whom they had been sent in search, and had returned to the yacht just in time to see her captured. He wound up his story with the remark that Chase and Wilson must have been secured, before he and Bab came within sight of the vessel, for they had seen nothing of them.

"Well, this is a pretty state of affairs," said Walter, as soon as he could speak. "Instead of assisting Fred Craven, we have managed to lose three more of our fellows. As far as I can see we are done for now, and all that is left us is to look about for a chance to go home. But first, I'd like to know what those men intend to do with the yacht. Do you see where they are going? Let's walk around the beach. I want to keep her in sight as long as I can, for I never expect to see her after to-night."

Walter did not keep the Banner in sight five minutes after he spoke. She had by this time reached the other side of the harbor, and disappeared among the trees and bushes that lined the shore, having probably entered a creek that flowed into the bay. With one accord the boys bent their steps along the beach toward the spot where she had last been seen, not with any intention of trying to recover possession of her, but simply because they did not know what else to do.

It was fully three miles around the beach to the woods in which the Banner had vanished from their view, but the boys had so much to talk about that the distance did not seem nearly so great. Almost before they were aware of it, they were stumbling about among the bushes, in close proximity to the Banner's hiding-place. Not deeming it policy to attract the attention of her crew, they ceased their conversation and became more cautious in their movements—a proceeding on which they had reason to congratulate themselves; for, before they had gone fifty yards farther, they saw the Banner's tall, taper masts rising through the bushes directly in advance of them. They looked about among the trees in every direction, but could see no one. They listened, but no sound came from the direction of the yacht. The same encouraging thought occurred to each of the boys at the same moment, and Eugene was the first to give utterance to it.

"Can it be possible, that the deserters have run her in here and left her?" he asked, excitedly.

"It is possible, but hardly probable," replied Walter. "They didn't steal her just to run her across the bay and leave her. They're going to Havana in her."

"I know that. But if they are on board, why don't we hear them talking or walking about? They may have gone back to the village for something."

"Then we should have met them," said Walter. "But, if you say so, we'll go up nearer and reconnoitre. I'd like to have one more look at the Banner, before I give her up for ever."

"Go on," said Perk. "If they are there, we need not show ourselves."

Walter, throwing himself on his hands and knees, crept cautiously toward the bank of the creek, and in a few minutes laid hold of the Banner's bob-stay, and drew himself to an erect position. The little vessel lay close alongside the bank, held by a single line, her bowsprit being run into the bushes. Her sails had been lowered, but were not furled, and this made it evident that her captors had either hurriedly deserted her, or that they intended very soon to get her under way again. The boys listened, but could hear no movement on the deck. Afraid to give utterance to the hopes that now arose in his mind, Walter looked toward his companions, and receiving an encouraging nod from each, seized the bob-stay again, and drawing himself up to the bowsprit, looked over the rail. There was no one in sight. Slowly and carefully he made his way to the deck, closely followed by Perk and Eugene, and presently they were all standing beside the hatch that led into the galley. It was open, and a close examination of the apartment below, showed them that it was empty. There was still one room to be looked into, and that was the cabin. If there was no one there, the Banner would be their own again in less than thirty seconds.

Without an instant's pause, Walter placed his hands on the combings of the hatch, and lowered himself through, still closely followed by his companions. The door leading into the cabin was closed but not latched. Slowly and noiselessly it yielded to the pressure of Walter's hand, and swung open so that the boys could obtain a view of the interior of the cabin. They looked, and all their hopes of recovering the yacht vanished on the instant. Lying in different attitudes about the cabin—stretched upon the lockers and on the floor, were five stalwart men, all fast asleep; and conspicuous among them was Pierre, the smuggler. Walter hastily closed the door, and without saying a word, began to remove the hatch that led into the hold.

"That's the idea," whispered Eugene. "We'll rescue Bab before we go ashore. Let me go down after him; I know he's there."

"We'll all go down," replied Walter; "and we'll not go ashore at all if we can help it. I, for one, don't intend to leave the yacht again until I am put off by a superior force. We'll do as Tomlinson and his crowd did—conceal ourselves in the hold until the Banner is so far out to sea that we can't be put off, and then we'll come out."

This was more than Perk and Eugene had bargained for. They believed it to be rather a reckless piece of business to trust themselves in the power of the new crew of the Banner. It was probably the best way to regain control of the yacht—the deserters would have no use for her after they reached Havana—but what if they should be angry when they found the boys aboard, and vent their spite by treating them harshly? In that event, they would be in a predicament indeed, for they could not get ashore, and neither could they defend themselves against the attacks of grown men. But if Walter was determined to stay, of course they would stay with him. If he got into trouble, they would be near him to share it; and there was some consolation in knowing that they could not get into much worse situations than those they had already passed through. They followed him when he lowered himself into the hold, and it was well they did so; for when Perk, who brought up the rear, was half way through the hatch, some one in the cabin uttered a loud yawn, and rising to his feet, approached the door leading into the galley. As quick as a flash, Perk dropped into the hold, closing the hatch after him; and immediately afterward, almost before he had time to draw another breath, the cabin door opened, and the man came in. The frightened and excited boys crouched close under the hatch, afraid to move for fear of attracting his attention. They heard him move something across the floor of the galley and step upon it; and they knew by the first words he uttered that it was Pierre, and that he was taking an observation of the weather.

"Roll out there, lads, and turn to!" he exclaimed. "By the time we get the yacht turned round, and the sails hoisted, it will be dark. We're going to have a cloudy, breezy night for our run, and that's just what we want. Come, bullies, make a break, there."

The order was followed by a general movement in the cabin, and the boys, believing that the sound of the heavy footsteps overhead would drown any noise they might make in moving about the hold, seized the opportunity to look up a place of concealment among the water-butts and tool-chests. Walter's first care, however, was to look, or rather feel for the lantern which he and his brother always used when visiting the hold. It was found hanging in its accustomed place. With the solitary match he happened to have in his pocket he lighted the wick, and the first object that was revealed to himself and companions was Bab, sitting with his hands tied behind him and his back against one of the water-butts. The prisoner, who, up to this time had believed that his visitors were some of the deserters, was too amazed to speak. Indeed he did not try until Eugene and Perk had untied his hands, and given him each a hearty slap on the back by way of greeting.

"All the merest accident in the world, my boy," said Eugene. "Such a thing never happened before and never will again. We never expected to see you on the yacht, either. Come up into this dark corner, and tell us what you know of the plans of these men. Hallo! what's this?"

While Eugene was speaking he was walking toward the after end of the hold. On the way he stumbled over something, which, upon examination, proved to be a long, narrow box, bearing upon its top a name and address: "DON CASPER NEVIS, Port Platte, Cuba."

"How did that box come here?" asked Walter,

"I never saw it before. And what are in those packages?" he added, pointing to a couple of bales that lay near by.

"Here's another box," continued Eugene, "and it is so heavy I can scarcely move it. There's some printing on it, too. Hold your lantern here."

Walter did as his brother requested, and he and the rest, who crowded about the box and looked over Eugene's shoulder, read the same name and address they had seen on the other box; and underneath, in smaller print were the words: "Percussion Cartridges."

"Now just listen to me a minute and I'll tell you what's a fact," said Perk. "Here are the bullets—I don't know how they came here, but they're *here*—and if we only had the guns to throw them, we could clear the yacht's deck of these interlopers in less time than it takes to tell it."

"Well, I declare!" exclaimed Walter suddenly, and in tones indicative of great surprise.

"Made any more discoveries?" asked Perk.

"I have," replied the young captain, who by the aid of his lantern, was closely scrutinizing the long box. "Here are the very things you are wishing for. Just listen to this: One dozen Spencer's army carbines."

The boys could scarcely believe their ears; they wanted the evidence of their eyes to back it up. With a volley of ejaculations, which in their excitement they uttered in tones altogether too loud, they gathered about the box, looked at the words Walter had read to them, then rubbed their eyes and looked again.

"Well, now I am beat," said Bab.

"I'd give something to know how these articles came here," observed Walter, deeply perplexed.

"Can it be possible that they were brought aboard by the deserters, who intend to start out on a piratical cruise on their own hook?" asked Perk.

While the three boys were discussing the matter in this way, Eugene, who was the first to recover himself, took the lantern from his brother's hand, and creeping forward to the carpenter's chest, soon returned with a screw-driver. While one held the light, and the others looked on, he set to work upon the long box, and presently the lid was removed and the interior disclosed to view. There they were, a half a dozen bran new breech-loaders, and under them were as many more of the same sort.

While Eugene was handing them out, Perk seized the screw-driver, and in five minutes more the cover of the ammunition box had been taken off, and four of the carbines were loaded and ready for use.

"Now, then, lead on, Walter!" exclaimed Eugene, triumphantly. " One rush, and she's ours. Won't those villians be surprised when they see the muzzles of four seven-shooters looking them squarely in the face? Why, fellows, they've got the yacht under sail already."

If Eugene had said that the Banner had left the creek behind, and was well on her way toward the entrance to the harbor, he would have been nearly right.

CHAPTER XII.

THE BANNER UNDER FIRE.

WHILE Walter and his friends were engaged in unpacking the boxes containing the carbines and ammunition, Pierre and his crew had been equally busy on deck. By the time they had turned the yacht around with her bow toward the mouth of the creek and hoisted the sails, it was pitch dark, and her captain determined to begin the voyage at once. The boys below were so intent upon their investigations, and so astonished at their discoveries, that they did not know that the yacht was in motion; but when she got out into the harbor where she felt the full force of the breeze, they speedily became aware of the fact, for the Banner, following her usual custom, rolled over until her front gunwale was almost level with the water, and Walter and his companions slid down to the lee side of the hold as easily as if the floor had been ice, and they mounted on skates. Shut out as they were from view of surrounding objects, and being beyond the reach of the voices of the men on deck, they were saved the anxiety and alarm they would have felt, had they known all that happened during the next half hour. They were in blissful ignorance of the fact that they were that night under fire for the first time in their lives, but such was the truth; and this was the way it came about.

Had Tomlinson and his men known all that Pierre knew, the voyage to Havana would never have been undertaken. The latter was well aware of the fact that more than one cargo of arms and ammunition had been smuggled into that very port for the use of the Cuban insurgents—he ought to have known it, for he belonged to the vessel engaged in the business—and he had also learned that the Stella was suspected, and that vigilant officers were keeping an eye on all her movements. He knew, further, that certain things had been done by Mr. Bell that afternoon, calculated to draw the attention of the Spanish officials, from the Stella to the Banner; that she would be closely watched; that she had been seen to cross the harbor and enter the creek; that an attempt would be made to board and search her before she left the port; and that in case the attempt failed, a Spanish frigate was close at hand to pursue her, and the fort on the point was ready to open fire upon her. But knowing all these things as well as he did, he was willing to attempt to smuggle the Banner out of the harbor, for he was working for money.

Hugging the shore as closely as the depth of the water would permit, the yacht sped on her way toward the point, the crew standing in silence at their posts, and Pierre himself handling the wheel. With the exception of the lamp in the binnacle, and the lantern in the hold which the boys were using, there was not a light about her, and no one spoke a word, not even in a whisper. But with all these precautions, the yacht did not leave the harbor unobserved. Just as she arrived off the point on which the fort was situated, a light suddenly appeared in her course. It came from a dark lantern. The man who carried it was the same officer who had boarded the vessel in the morning, and who, for reasons of his own, had made the young sailors believe that he could not speak their language. He was standing in the stern-sheets of a large yawl, which was filled with armed men, ready to board the yacht, when she came to, in obedience to his hail.

"Banner ahoy!" yelled the officer, in as plain English as Walter himself could have commanded.

"There they are, cap'n," whispered Tomlinson, who had been stationed in the bow to act as lookout. "A cutter, and a dozen men in her. Are you going to answer the hail?"

"Leave all that to me. Come here and take the wheel, and hold her just as she is," said Pierre; and when Tomlinson obeyed the order, the new captain hurried to the rail, and looked toward the yawl.

"Banner ahoy!" shouted the officer again, as the schooner flew past his boat.

"Yaw! Vat you want?" answered Pierre, imitating as nearly as he could the broken English of a German.

"Lie to!" commanded the officer.

"Vas?" yelled Pierre.

"Lie to, I say. I want to come aboard of you."

"Nix forstay!"

"That won't go down, my friend; I know you," said the officer, angrily. "Give away, strong," he added, addressing himself to his crew. "You had better stop and let me come aboard."

Pierre seemed very anxious to understand. He moved aft as the Banner went on, leaving the boat behind, and even leaned as far as he could over the taffrail, and placed his hand behind his ear as if trying to catch the officer's words. But he did not stop; he knew better. The boat followed the yacht a short distance, and then turned and went swiftly toward the point, the officer waving his lantern in air as if making signals to some one. When Pierre saw that, he knew there were exciting times ahead.

"Give me the wheel, now," said he; "and do you go for'ard and heave the lead until I tell you to stop. Station a man in the waist to pass the word, and tell him not to speak too loud. Tell two others to stand by the sheets, and send Bob aloft to unfurl the topsails. We have need of all the rags we can spread now."

"What's up?" asked Tomlinson, with some anxiety.

"There'll be a good deal up if we don't get away from here in a hurry," replied Pierre; "more than you think for. But if you do as I tell you, I will bring you through all right. That fort will open on us in less than five minutes, and if that don't stop us, we'll have to run a race with a man o' war."

Tomlinson waited to hear no more. Resigning the wheel into Pierre's hands, he ran forward, and the latter, as soon as the men had been stationed at the fore and main sheets, changed the yacht's course, heading her across a bar at the entrance to the harbor, and standing close along shore. The wisdom of this manœuvre was very soon made apparent. In less than ten minutes afterward, there was a bright flash behind them, accompanied by a shrieking sound in the air, and a twelve pound shell went skipping along the waves and burst far in advance of the yacht. Had she been in the channel, which vessels of large size were obliged to follow in going in and out of the harbor, she would have been directly in range of it. Another and another followed, and finally every gun on the seaward side of the fort was sending its missiles in the direction the Banner was supposed to have gone. The deserters looked and listened in amazement; but finding that they were out of reach of the shells, their alarm began to abate.

"Now, this is like old times," exclaimed Bob, placing his left hand behind his back, extending his right, and glancing along the yacht's rail, in the attitude of the captain of a gun when about to pull the lock-string. "Don't I wish this craft was the old Indianola, as good as she was the day she ran the batteries at Vicksburg, and I had one of those eleven-inch guns under my eye, loaded with a five-second shell?"

"You'll wish for her many a time to-night, for the fun isn't over yet," observed Pierre. "It is only just beginning. Now keep silence, fore and aft, so that I can hear what Tom has to say about the water."

For an hour Tomlinson kept heaving the lead, passing the word back to Pierre with every throw, and all this while the Banner, with every inch of her canvas spread, bounded along as close to the shore as her captain dared to go. For fifteen minutes of this time the fort continued to send its shots and shells along the channel, and then the firing ceased and all was still again. Pierre kept close watch of the shore as the yacht flew along, and finally turning into a little bay, sailed up within sight of a stone jetty that put out from the shore, and came to anchor. This was Don Casper's wharf Pierre knew it, for he had often been there; and he knew too that a short distance away, among the negro quarters, was a storehouse containing an abundance of corn-meal, flour and bacon. This was the place to secure the provisions.

"There!" exclaimed the captain, as the Banner swung around with her head to the waves, "we're so far on our way to Havana, and we haven't been long getting here, either. Now we've no time to lose. Who's the best swimmer in the party?"

"I am," said Tomlinson confidently.

"Well, then, come here. Do you see that wharf out there, and the yawls lying alongside of it? Just swim out and bring one of 'em back, and we'll go ashore and get the grub. Be in a hurry, for we want to get our business done and put to sea again before that man-o'-war comes up and blockades us."

Tomlinson at once divested himself of his peajacket, overshirt and shoes, and plunging fearlessly into the waves made his way to the shore. While there, notwithstanding Pierre's suggestion that haste was desirable, he took it into his head to reconnoitre the plantation. He found the storehouse, and saw the overseer—the same man who liberated Chase and Wilson from the wine-cellar—serving out provisions to the negroes. After noting the position of the building, so that he could easily find it again, he secured one of the yawls, hoisted a sail in it, and returning to the yacht brought off his companions. Pierre knowing more than the deserters, and believing that it might not be quite safe to trust himself too far away from the yacht, remained at the wharf, while Tomlinson and the rest of the deserters, armed with handspikes which they had brought from the vessel, went to the storehouse after the provisions.

And what were the boys in the hold doing all this while? They would not have believed that a full hour and a half had elapsed since they discovered and liberated Bab, for they were busy and the time flew quickly by. In the first place, each boy crammed his pockets full of cartridges and took possession of one of the carbines, and the rest were carefully hidden among the ballast, for fear that they might by some accident fall into the hands of the deserters. When this had been done, Eugene, with his usual impetuosity and lack of prudence, began to urge an immediate attack upon the captors of the yacht; but Walter and Perk thought it best to adhere to the original plan, and keep themselves concealed until the yacht was well out to sea, or, at all events, until she was clear of the harbor. They argued that when the attack was made it would produce something of a commotion on deck, which might attract the attention of the crews of some of the neighboring vessels, and perhaps of the Spanish officials; and, although the Banner was their own property, and they had as good a right in Cuba as any of their countrymen, they did not wish to be called upon to make any explanations. Bab sided with Walter and Perk, and Eugene was obliged to yield. It was well that he did not carry his point, for had the lawful captain of the yacht been in command when she was hailed by the revenue officer, he would have obeyed the order to lie to, and he and his crew would have been carried back to town and thrown into jail as smugglers. The officer would have found proof against them too; and such proof as Walter knew nothing about.

It being decided at last that Walter's plan was the best, the boys, in order to gratify their curiosity, proceeded to examine the contents of the bales they had found in the hold. The first contained artillery sabres, and Eugene buckled one about his waist;

but the others declined to follow his example, believing that the carbines were all the weapons they needed. The other two packages contained officers' sashes, one of which Eugene also appropriated. While thus engaged they heard the roar of the guns from the fort, but they little dreamed that they were pointed in the direction the yacht was supposed to have gone. Shut in as they were on all sides by tight wooden walls, the sound seemed to them to come from a great distance. They accounted for the firing in various ways—the soldiers were rejoicing over some decisive victory the Spaniards had gained over the insurgents; or they were engaged in artillery practice; or perhaps a skirmish was going on back of the town. So little interested were they in the matter, that, after the first few shots, they ceased to pay any attention to the noise. They had their own affairs to think and talk about: what could have become of Chase and Wilson—they had searched the hold without finding any traces of them—and who had brought the arms and ammunition aboard? Where had Fred Craven and his keepers gone so suddenly? and what should be done with the unlawful crew of the yacht after they had been secured? By the time these points had been talked over, the Banner had accomplished the ten miles that lay between the harbor and the bay at the rear of Don Casper's plantation, and then Walter declared that Pierre and Tomlinson had had charge of the vessel long enough, and that it was time he was claiming his rights again. The boys were ready to move at the word. It was a novel and perhaps desperate thing they were about to undertake, but not one of them hesitated. Grasping their weapons with a firmer hold, they followed closely after Walter, and gathered silently about him as he stopped under the hatch.

"Are we all ready?" asked the young commander, in an excited whisper. "I will throw off the hatch, and, Bab, be sure you are ready to hand me my carbine the moment I jump out. If any of the deserters hear the noise and come into the galley to see what is going on, I will keep them at bay until you come up. If we find them on deck, let each fellow pick out a man, cover him with his gun, and order him into the hold."

"Yes, and see that he goes, too," added Eugene.

"Perk, blow out that lantern. Stand by, fellows!"

The boys crouched like so many tigers ready for

a spring; but just as Walter placed his hands upon the hatch, preparatory to throwing it off, a few harshly spoken words of command came faintly to their ears, followed by the rattling of the chain through the hawse hole, and a sudden cessation of motion, telling the young sailors that the yacht had come to anchor. This caused Walter to hesitate; and after a few whispered words with his companions, they all sat down on the floor of the hold under the hatch to await developments. But nothing new transpired. The yacht was as silent as the grave; and after half an hour of inactivity, the patience of the young tars was all exhausted, and once more preparations were made for the attack. Walter handed his carbine to Bab, and lifting the hatch quickly, but noiselessly, from its place, swung himself out of the hold into the galley. The others followed with all possible haste, and when the last one had come out, Walter pushed open the door of the cabin and rushed in. The room was empty. Without a moment's pause, he ran toward the standing room, and when he got there, found himself in undisputed possession of his vessel, no one being on deck to oppose him. The yacht was deserted by all save himself and companions. The young tars, scarcely able to realize the fact, hurried about, peeping into all sorts of improbable places, and when at last they had satisfied themselves that the deserters were really gone, their joy knew no bounds.

"It's all right, fellows!" cried Walter, gleefully. "She's ours, and we've got her without a fight, too. I have some curiosity to know where those men have gone, but we'll not stop to inquire. Stand by to get under way."

"Shall I slip the cable?" asked Eugene.

"No," answered Walter. "I can't see the beauty of throwing away a good chain and anchor when there's no occasion for it. Let's man the capstan."

While two of the crew busied themselves in removing the chain from the bitts to the little horizontal capstan with which the yacht was provided, the others brought the handspikes from their places, and presently the schooner began walking slowly up to her anchor. The boys worked manfully, and presently Eugene looked over the bow and announced that the anchor was apeak.

"Go to the wheel, Perk," said Walter. "Heave away, the rest of us. Cheerily, lads!"

Perk at once hurried aft, but just as he laid his hand on the wheel he stopped short, gazed intently over the stern toward the shore, and then quietly made his way forward again. "Now I'll tell you what's a fact," he whispered; "you'd better work that capstan a little livelier, for they're coming."

"Who are coming?" asked all the boys at once.

"Well, there's a yawl close aboard of us, and if you can tell who is in it, you will do more than I can."

The young sailors looked in the direction Perk pointed, and saw a sailboat swiftly approaching the yacht. To heave the anchor clear of the ground and get under way before she came alongside, was impossible, for she was already within a few rods of the vessel.

"Stand by to keep them off," said Walter, catching up his carbine. "We don't want to hurt any of them if we can help it, but bear in mind that they must not, under any circumstances, be allowed to come over the side."

The boys, with their weapons in their hands, hurried to the rail, and Walter was on the point of hailing the boat, and warning the deserters that any attempt to board the yacht would be stubbornly resisted, when he discovered that she had but one occupant. The others became aware of the fact at the same moment, and Eugene declared that it was none other than Pierre Coulte. "Let him come aboard, fellows," he added, "and we'll make him tell where Featherweight went to-day in such a hurry. We may learn something to our advantage."

Before his companions had time either to consent to, or reject this proposition, the yawl rounded to under the bow of the Banner, and a head appeared above the rail. The boys crouched close to the deck, and in a few seconds more a human figure leaped into view, and after looking all about the yacht, ran toward the capstan. On his way he passed within reach of Walter, who thrust out both his sinewy arms, and wrapping them about the intruder's legs, prostrated him in an instant. No sooner had he touched the deck than Perk, who was always on the alert, threw himself across the man's shoulders, and seizing both his hands, held them fast.

The stranger lay for an instant overcome with surprise at this unexpected reception, and then began to show his disapproval by the most frantic struggles; and although he was firmly held, he gave evidence of possessing uncommon strength and determination. But it was not Pierre they had got hold of, as they quickly discovered. There was something about him that reminded them of somebody else. Perk, at least, thought so, for he bent his head nearer to the stranger's, remarking as he did so:

"Now I'll tell you what's a fact—"

When he had said this much he paused, and started as if he had been shot, for a familiar voice interrupted him with—

"I say, Perk, if that's you, you needn't squeeze all the breath out of me."

"Wilson!" cried the crew of the Banner, in concert.

Perk jumped to his feet, pulling the prisoner up with him. It was Wilson and no mistake.

CHAPTER XIII.

THE SPANISH FRIGATE.

"HOW came you here?" was of course the first question the Club addressed to the new-comer, as soon as they had made sure of his identity.

"I came in that boat," replied Wilson, who was quite as much surprised to see his friends as they were to see him. "But how did *you* come here? I heard Tomlinson say that he and his crowd had stolen the Banner."

"So they did; but they stole us with her, for we were hidden in the hold. What we want to know is, how you happen to be out here in the country. We left you and Chase to watch the yacht."

"It is a long story, fellows, and I will tell it to you the first chance I get. But just how we have something else to think of. There comes Pierre," said Wilson, pointing over the stern. "He is after me. Tomlinson and the rest are ashore stealing some provisions."

"Does Pierre know where Featherweight is?" asked Eugene.

"I should'nt wonder. He seems to be pretty well acquainted with Mr. Bell's plans."

"Then we will see if we can make him tell them to us," said Walter. "Eugene, go down and get a lantern; and the rest of us stand by to receive our visitor with all the honors."

"Why, where did you get this?" asked Wilson, as Eugene placed his carbine in his hands.

"'Thereby hangs a tale;' but you shall hear it in due time."

"Here he is, fellows," whispered Walter. "Keep out of sight until he comes over the side."

Pierre was by this time close aboard of the schooner. He came up under her stern, and sprang over the rail with the yawl's painter in his hand. "I told you that you shouldn't go off in this vessel," said he, looking about the deck in search of Wilson. 'You needn't think to hide from me, for I am bound to find you. You will save yourself some rough handling by getting into this yawl and going straight back to shore. We don't want you here."

"But we want you," exclaimed Walter, starting up close at Pierre's side and presenting his carbine full in his face.

The others jumped from their concealments, and at the same moment Eugene opened the door of the cabin and came out into the standing-room with a lighted lantern in his hand. For a few seconds the smuggler was so completely blinded by the glare of the bull's-eye, which Eugene turned full upon him, that he could not distinguish even the nearest objects; but presently his eyes became somewhat accustomed to the light, and he was able to take a view of his surroundings. He was much astonished at what he saw. There stood Wilson, whom he had expected to drag from some concealment, looking very unlike the cringing, supplicating youth he had met on the jetty. And he was not alone either, for with him were the boys whom he believed he had left ten miles behind him, and also Bab, whom he had last seen bound and helpless in the hold. They were all armed too, and were holding their cocked guns in most unpleasant proximity to his face.

"Well, if you have anything to say for yourself let's have it," said Wilson, breaking the silence at last. "You'll let me go off in this vessel after all, won't you? There's a good fellow."

Pierre had not a word to say. He seemed to be overcome with bewilderment and alarm. He did not even remonstrate, when Eugene, after placing his lantern on the deck, stepped up, and passing a rope around his arms confined them behind his back. When the operation of tying him was completed, he seemed to arouse himself as if from a sound sleep, and to realize for the first time that he was a prisoner; but then it was too late to resist even if he had the inclination. The knowledge of this fact did not, however, appear to occasion him any uneasiness. As soon as the first tremor, caused by the sight of the cocked weapons, passed away, he began to recover his courage.

"There," said Eugene, taking another round turn with the rope, "I think that will hold you. Didn't I tell you that you would never get far away with the yacht? You're fast enough now."

"But I'll not be so long," replied Pierre, with a grin. "There's a man-of-war coming, if you only knew it, and she'll be along directly."

"Well, what of it?"

"Nothing much, only she will take you and your

vessel, and set me at liberty; that's all. She is looking for you."

"She is? We don't care. We've done nothing to make us afraid of her."

"You'd better be afraid of her," replied Pierre, significantly. "You've got no papers."

"Yes, I have," interrupted Walter.

"How does that come?" asked Pierre, in a tone of voice that was aggravating to the last degree. "Did you clear from Port Platte?"

"No, because we didn't get the chance. You stole the vessel and run away with her. But I can show that we cleared from Bellville."

"No, you can't. And, more than that, you've got guns and ammunition aboard intended for the use of the Cubans."

Pierre paused when he said this, and looked at the boys as if he expected them to be very much astonished; and they certainly were. They knew now where the carbines came from, and why they had been placed in the hold, and their words and actions indicated that if the guilty party had been within their reach just then, he would have fared roughly indeed. Walter was the only one who had nothing to say. He stood for a moment as mute and motionless as if he had been turned into stone, and then catching up the lantern, rushed into his cabin. He opened his desk, and with nervous haste began to overhaul the papers it contained.

"O, you'll not find them there," said Pierre, "they're gone—torn up, and scattered about the harbor."

"What's the matter, Walter?" asked all the boys at once.

"Our papers are gone, that's all," replied the young captain, calmly. "Some one has stolen them. Now, Pierre," he added, paying no heed to the exclamations of rage and astonishment that arose on all sides, "I want you to tell me what has been going on on board my vessel this afternoon."

"Well, I don't mind obliging you," answered the smuggler, "seeing that it is too late for you to repair the damage, and, in order to make you understand it, I must begin at the beginning. You see, although we cleared from Bellville for Havana, we did not intend to go there at all. This very bay is the point we were bound for, but it is an ugly place in a gale, and so we put into Port Platte to wait until the wind and sea went down, so that we could land our cargo. Perhaps you don't know it, but the Stella is loaded with just such weapons as these you've got."

"I don't doubt it," said Walter, "but why did you bring some of them aboard this vessel?"

"I'll come to that directly. When you set out in pursuit of us, after we left Lost Island, we knew that you must have found Chase, and that he had told you the whole story; but we didn't feel at all uneasy, for we believed that when we once lost sight of you we should never see you again. As bad luck would have it, however, the storm blew you right into Port Platte, and of course you found us there. When we saw you come in we knew what you wanted to do, and set our wits at work to get the start of you, and I rather think we've done it. We laid half a dozen plans, believing that if one failed another would be sure to work. In the first place Mr. Bell directed the attention of the custom-house officers to you and your vessel. He is well acquainted with them all, you know, and he has fooled them more than once, as nicely as he fooled the captain of that cutter at Lost Island. He told them that you were the fellows who were smuggling all the arms into this country for the use of the rebels; that you had intended to land somewhere on the coast, but had been compelled by the gale to come into the harbor, and that you would probably go out again as soon as the wind died away. Having excited the officers' suspicions, the next thing was to do something to back them up; and we thought the best way would be to smuggle some weapons aboard the Banner. But in order to do it we had to work some plan to get you away from the yacht, so that we could have a clear field for our operations. Mr. Bell and Captain Conway took Fred Craven up the hill in plain sight of you, and, as we expected, some of you followed him. Then the mate found one of Don Casper's niggers on the wharf, and used him to help his plans along. He wrote a note to Chase, and signed Walter's name to it."

"Aha!" interrupted Wilson. "I begin to see into things a little. But how did Mr. Bell know that Chase was left in command of the yacht?"

"He didn't know it—he only guessed it from seeing him so active in setting things to rights."

"Don Casper," repeated Perk. "His name is on those boxes in the hold. Who is he?"

"He's the man to whom we deliver our weapons, and he sends them to the rebels. As I was saying,

Mr. Bell wrote this note to Chase, asking him to bring all the crew of the vessel to assist in releasing Fred, and another to Don Casper, and hired the darkey to deliver them and take the boys out to the Don's in his wagon. But when the mate, who had the management of the affair, reached the yacht, he found that Tomlinson and his crowd, whom he supposed to be visitors from some neighboring vessel, were a part of the crew, and of course he had to get rid of them in some way; so he invited them down to the Stella to get breakfast. Then he went back, gave the negro the notes, and he took Chase and Wilson out to Don Casper's. After that, the mate returned to the yacht, and taking some arms and ammunition, stowed them away on board the yacht, and wound up by stealing your clearance papers, which Mr. Bell destroyed."

"And much good may the act do him," exclaimed Eugene, angrily.

"All's fair in war," replied Pierre. "You came here to get us into trouble, and of course if we could beat you at your own game, we had a perfect right to do it."

"No, you hadn't," retorted Wilson. "We were engaged in lawful business, and you were not."

"No matter; we make our living by it. As time passed, and you did not come back and sail out so that the officers could board you—"

"But why were you so very anxious to have us go out?" asked Walter. "Simply because you wanted us captured?"

"Well—no; we had something else in view. You see, we were in a great hurry to go up to the Don's and land our weapons, but we had a suspicion that some sharp eyes were watching us and our vessel. Mr. Bell knew by the way the officers acted, that they hadn't quite made up their minds which vessel it was that was carrying the contraband goods—The Stella or the Banner. They didn't like to search us, for they didn't want to believe anything wrong of Mr. Bell—they had known him so long and were such good friends of his; just like the captain of that cutter, you know. But yet they couldn't believe that your yacht was the smuggler, for she didn't look like one. We wanted the officers to find the arms on board your vessel; and until that event happened, we were afraid to ask for a clearance—that's the plain English of it. Well, as you didn't come back and take the yacht out, and Mr. Bell was very anxious that she should go, he thought it best to change his plans a little. Learning that Tomlinson and his friends had come to Cuba to ship aboard a privateer, he hired me to join in with them and steal the Banner. He told me that it would be a desperate undertaking, for the officers were all eyes and ears, the fort was ready to open fire on the yacht if she tried to slip out, and if that didn't stop her, a frigate was near by to capture her. But he offered me a hundred dollars to do the job, and I agreed to smuggle her out. I did it, too. The fort fired more than fifty shots after us—"

"It did!" ejaculated Eugene.

"Were those guns we heard pointed at my vessel —at *us*?" demanded Walter, in a trembling voice.

"Not exactly at us, but in the direction we were supposed to have gone. I brought her through all right, however, and I can take her safely away from under the very guns of the frigate; but you can't do it, and I am glad of—"

"Take this man into the hold and shut him up there!" cried Walter, almost beside himself, with indignation and alarm. "I don't want to hear another word from him."

"O, you needn't mind those things," said Pierre,

as Perk and Bab picked up their carbines. "I am willing to go, but I shan't stay there long. You are as good as captured by that frigate already."

"Take him away!" shouted Walter. "Stay here, Perk, I want to talk to you."

The young captain began nervously pacing the deck, while the other boys marched their prisoner through the cabin into the galley, and assisted him rather roughly into the hold. They placed him with his back against one of the water-butts, and while Eugene was looking for a rope with which to confine his feet, Wilson began to question him: "Since you have shown yourself so obliging," said he, "perhaps you won't mind telling me what was in the note that darkey gave to Don Casper."

"There wasn't much," was the reply. "It was written by Captain Conway, who told the Don that the bearers were members of his crew, and that he had sent them out there to make arrangements with him about landing our cargo of arms."

"Well, go on. You said you sent Chase and me to the Don's, on purpose to have us captured by the Spaniards."

"We thought that perhaps we might get rid of you in that way. We know that the Don is sus pected, and we believe that if strangers, and Americans too, were seen going there in the daytime, they would get themselves into trouble."

"We came very near it," said the boy, drawing a long breath when he thought of all that had passed at the plantation, "but the Don took care of us."

"Tell us all about it, Wilson," said Eugene, coming aft with the rope at this moment. "By the way, where is Chase? I haven't seen anything of him."

Wilson replied that he hadn't seen him either very recently. He hoped that he was all right, but he feared the worst, for he was still ashore, and might fall into the hands of the Spaniards. And then he went on to relate, in a few hurried words, the adventures that had befallen him since he left the yacht at the wharf, to all of which Pierre listened attentively, now and then manifesting his satisfaction by broad grins. There were two things he could not understand, Wilson said, in conclusion: one was, how the Don escaped being made a prisoner when the patrol surrounded the house, and the other, where Chase went in such a hurry. In regard to the missing boy we will here remark, that none of our young friends knew what had become of him until several months afterward, and then they met him very unexpectedly, and in a place where they least imagined they would see him. The mystery of the Don's escape was no mystery after all. When he locked the boys in their place of concealment, he made his exit from the house through one of the cellar windows, and hid himself in a thicket of evergreens beside the back verandah. Watching his opportunity when the soldiers were busy searching the building, he crept quietly away and took refuge in one of the negro cabins. He kept a sharp eye on the movements of the patrol, and saw that those who left the house took several riderless horses with them. This made it evident that some of their number were still on the premises, and that they had remained to arrest the Don when he came back. But of course he did not go back. As soon as it grew dark his overseer brought him his cloak and weapons, and then returning to the house, succeeded in releasing the boys, as we have described.

"Now, Pierre, there's another thing that perhaps you wouldn't object to explaining," said Eugene, when he had finished tying the prisoner's feet. "Didn't Mr. Bell know that you and your father took Chase to Lost Island in a dugout?"

"Of course he did."

"What did you do with the pirogue?"

"We chopped her up and put her into the fire. That's the reason you couldn't find her."

"How did you get aboard the Stella? We didn't see you, and we watched her all the time."

"Not all the time, I guess. There were a few minutes while you were searching The Kitchen that you didn't have your eyes on her, and during that time pap and me came out of the bushes and boarded her. Mr. Bell knew very well that if you could have your own way you would get him into a scrape, and so he put a bold face on the matter, and bluffed you square down."

While the boys were asking one another if there were any other points they wanted Pierre to explain, they heard a voice calling to them through the hatchway. It was Perk's voice; and when they answered his summons, they were surprised to see that his face was pale with excitement, and that he was trembling in every limb. "Hurry up, fellows," he whispered. "She's coming."

"Who is?"

"The frigate. We can see her lights. Walter

is going to give her the slip if he can, and go back to the village."

"Aha!" exclaimed Pierre who caught the words. "What did I tell you? It will do you no good to go to town, for Mr. Bell will be on hand with proof to back up all his charges."

Without waiting to hear what Pierre had to say, the boys sprang out of the hold, slamming the hatch after them. Walter met them in the standing room, and issued his orders with a calmness that surprised them. He sent Bab to the wheel, and with the others went to work to cat and fish the anchor, which, with a few turns of the capstan was heaved clear of the ground. As busy as they were, they found time now and then to cast their eyes toward the Gulf. There were the lights that had excited Walter's alarm, in plain sight; and the fact that they stood high above the water, and that the waves communicated but little motion to them, was conclusive evidence that they were suspended from the catheads of some large and heavy vessel. Beyond a doubt, the approaching craft was the iron-clad frigate they had seen in the harbor of Port Platte.

Never before had our heroes been placed in a

situation like this. Conscious that they had done nothing wrong, they felt that they were playing the part of cowards, and disgracing themselves by running away from the frigate, instead of boldly advancing to meet her. But the young captain, and his counsellor, Perk, did not know what else to do. Had the crew of the man-of-war been composed of his own countrymen, or had they been even honorable people, who would accord to him the treatment that civilized belligerents usually extend to their prisoners, the case would have been different. In spite of the evidence against him, Walter, feeling strong in his innocence, would fearlessly have surrendered himself and vessel; but he was afraid of the Spaniards, and he had good reason to be. They were so vindictive, cruel and unreasonable. Men who could deliberately shoot down a party of young students, for no other offence than defacing a monument, were not to be trusted. The longer Walter pondered the matter, the more alarmed he became.

"All gone, Bab," he exclaimed, as the anchor was pulled clear of the ground and the Banner began to drift toward the beach, "fill away, and get all you can out of her. Heave that lead, Eugene, and use it lively, for I don't know how much water there is here, and we must keep as close to the shore as we possibly can."

By the time the anchor was taken care of, the Banner was flying along the beach through darkness so intense that the anxious young captain, who perched himself upon the bow to act as lookout, could scarcely see a vessel's length ahead of him. There was now one question that was uppermost in his mind, and it was one to which time only could furnish a solution: Was the entrance to the bay wide or narrow? Upon this their safety depended. If they could get so far away from the frigate that they could slip by her in the darkness unperceived, their escape could be easily accomplished; but if they were obliged to pass within reach of the sharp eyes of her crew, their capture was certain. With his feelings worked up to the highest pitch of excitement, but to all outward appearances as calm as a summer morning, Walter awaited the issue.

The Banner bounded along as silently as if she had been a phantom yacht. She seemed to know the desperate situation of her crew. Every inch of the canvas was spread, the top-masts bent like fishing-rods under the weight of the heavy sails, and Bab now and then cast an anxious eye aloft, mo-

The "Banner."

mentarily expecting to see one of them give away under the unusual strain. But every rope held as if additional strength had been imparted to it. Not a block creaked; the tiller-rope, which usually groaned so loudly, gave out no sound as Bab moved the wheel back and forth; and even the water which boiled up under the bows, and now and then came on deck by buckets-full, gave out a faint, gurgling sound, as if it too sympathized with the boy crew. Ten minutes passed, and then Walter, who was watching the lights through his night-glass, stooped and whispered a few words to Wilson. The latter hurried aft and repeated them to Bab, and a moment later the yacht came up into the wind and lay like a log on the waves, drifting stern foremost toward the beach. The lights were scarcely a hundred yards distant. Nearer and nearer they came, and presently a high, black hull loomed up through the darkness, and moved swiftly past the yacht into the the bay. The young sailors held their breath in suspense, some closely watching the huge mass, which seemed almost on the point of running them down, others turning away their heads that they might not see it, and all listening for the hail from her deck which should announce their discovery.

But the frigate was as silent as if she had been deserted. She was not more than a minute in passing the yacht, and then she faded out of sight as quickly as she had come into view. Her captain did not expect to find the smuggler in the Gulf, but in the bay, and in the act of discharging her contraband cargo; and to this alone the Banner owed her escape.

As soon as the frigate was out of sight, Wilson carried another whispered order to Bab, and once more the Banner went bounding along the shore. It may have been all imagination on the part of her crew, and it doubtless was, but every one of them was ready to declare that she moved as if she felt easier after her narrow escape. The blocks creaked, the tiller-rope groaned as usual, the masts cracked and snapped, and the water under the bow roared and foamed like a miniature Niagara. Her company, one and all, breathed as if a mountain had been removed from their shoulders, but there were no signs of exultation among them. Their danger had been too great for that.

"Now just listen to me a minute, and I'll tell you what's a fact," said Perk, who was the first to find his tongue. "If you were a smuggler, Walter, you soon get up a reputation, and you would bother the custom-house fellows more than Captain Conway ever did. He couldn't do a neater trick than that, if he is an old—"

Crack! went something over their heads, with a report like that of a pistol, bringing Perk's congratulations to a sudden close, and startling every boy who heard it. Before they had time to look aloft there was another crash, and the main-topmast, with the sail attached, fell over to leeward, and flapped wildly in the wind. The backstay had parted, and of course the mast went by the board.

"Thank goodness! it held until we were out of danger," said Walter, as soon as he had made himself acquainted with the nature of the accident. "A crash like that, when the frigate was alongside, would have settled matters for us in a hurry."

Perk and Wilson at once went aloft to clear away the wreck, and Walter, being left to himself, began thoughtfully pacing the deck. Now that all danger from the frigate was passed, he had leisure to ponder upon that which was yet to come. What would be done with him and his companions when they gave themselves up to the authorities of the port? Would they believe their story? If the yacht had been supplied with the provisions necessary for the voyage to Bellville he would not have run the risk. He would have filled away for home without the loss of a moment. He had half a mind to try it any how. While he was turning the matter over in his mind, Eugene announced that there were more lights ahead of them.

"We had better get out our own lanterns," said the young commander. "There's no fun in rushing with almost railroad speed through such darkness as this. Some craft might run us down."

While the captain and his brother were employed in getting out the lights and hanging them to the catheads, Perk called out from the cross-trees, where he was busy with the broken mast: "I say, Walter, there's another frigate coming."

"How do you know?"

"Well, she may not be a frigate, but she wants to come alongside of us. I watched her, and just as soon as our lights were hung out she changed her course. She's coming toward us."

"I don't care," said Walter, now beginning to get discouraged. "We might as well give up one time as another. I shan't try to get out of her way."

The captain took his stand by Bab's side, and in order to satisfy himself that Perk was right, changed the course of the yacht several times, narrowly watching the approaching lights as he did so. Their position also changed, showing that the vessel intended to come up with her if possible. Being at last convinced of this fact, Walter walked forward again, and in moody silence waited to see what was going to happen.

CHAPTER XIV.

THE YACHT LOOKOUT.

"I AM disposed of at last, am I? I rather think not. I have the free use of my hands and feet, and if there's any opening in this state-room large enough for a squirrel to squeeze through, I shall be out of here in less than five minutes. There's the transom; I'll try that."

Thus spoke Fred Craven, who, with his hands in his pockets, was standing in the middle of his new prison, listening to the retreating footsteps of the men who had just placed him there. He had heard Captain Conway's sigh of relief, and caught the words he uttered when the door was locked upon him, and his soliloquy showed what he thought of the matter. He had not met with a single adventure during his captivity among the smugglers. Shortly after the Stella sailed from Lost Island he was released from the hold, and allowed the freedom of the deck. He messed with the crew, and, for want of some better way of passing the time, performed the duties of foremast hand as regularly and faithfully as though he had shipped for the voyage. He saw nothing of Mr. Bell, who remained in his cabin day and night, and had but little to say to any of the schooner's company. His mind was constantly occupied with thoughts of escape, and on more than one occasion, during the silence of the mid-watch, had he crept stealthily from his bunk in the forecastle and taken his stand by the rail, looking out at the angry waves which tossed the schooner so wildly about, hardly able to resist an insane desire to seize a life-buoy or handspike and spring into them. But prudence always stepped in in time to prevent him from doing anything rash, and finally curbing his impatience as well as he could he accepted the situation, working hard to keep his thoughts from wandering back to his home and friends, and constantly cheered by the hope that when once the shores of Cuba were sighted something would turn up in his favor. But he was doomed to disappointment. No sooner had the headlands at the entrance to the harbor of Port Platte appeared in view than he was ordered into the hold by Captain Conway, and secured beyond all possibility of escape. In the afternoon, however, he was again brought out, and, after listening to a long speech from Mr. Bell, the object of which was to make known to him the fact that he was to be taken ashore, and that his bodily comfort depended upon his observing the strictest silence, he was compelled to accompany him and the captain up the hill toward the village.

Featherweight thought he was now about to be turned over to the Spanish sea-captain, and so he was (only the captain, as it turned out, was an American who, for money, had undertaking to land Fred in some remote corner of the world); but first he had a part to perform, and that was to entice the crew of the Banner ashore in pursuit of him. As he slowly mounted the hill, he cast his eyes toward the Gulf, thinking the while of the quiet, pleasant little home, and the loving hearts he had left so far beyond it, and was greatly astonished to see a vessel, which looked exactly like the Banner, coming in. He did not know what had happened in the cove at Lost Island, and neither had he dreamed that Walter and his crew, bent on releasing him, had followed him for more than six hundred miles through a storm, the like of which they had never experienced before. He had not now the faintest idea that such was the case. What then must have been his amazement when he saw the vessel which had attracted his attention, haul suddenly into the shore and deposit Walter and Perk on the wharf? He saw the two boys as they followed him up the hill, and waved his handkerchief to them; and knowing just how courageous and determined they were, made up his mind that the moment of his deliverance was not far distant. But once more his hopes were dashed to the ground. His captors concealed themselves and him in a doorway until the pursuers had passed, and then the captain conducted him on board the ship and gave him into the hands of his new jailer. But Fred was resolved that he would not stay there. The ship was lying alongside the wharf; he was not bound, and if he could only work his way out of the state-room, it would be an easy matter to jump through one of the cabin windows into the water, and strike out for shore. The knowledge that there were friends at no great distance, ready and willing to assist him, encouraged him to make the attempt. There was not a moment to be lost. Mr. Bell had taken up more than two

17

hours by his manœuvres on shore; it was beginning to grow dark, the captain and all his crew were busy getting the ship under way, and the effort must be made before she left the wharf.

The first thing to which Fred directed his attention, was the transom—a narrow window over the door, opening into the cabin—and the next, a huge sea-chest which was stowed away under the bunk. To drag this chest from its place, and tip it upon one end under the transom, was an operation which did not occupy many minutes of time. When he sprang upon it, he found that his head was on a level with the window. There was no one in the cabin. With a beating heart he turned the button, but that was as far as he could go—an obstacle appeared. His new jailer had neglected no precautions for his safe keeping, for the transom was screwed down.

"Well, what of it?" soliloquized Featherweight, not in the least disheartened by this discovery. "There's more than one way to do things. I have the advantage of being smaller than most fellows of my age, and I can make my way through cracks in which an ordinary boy would stick fast. I believe

I could even get through the key-hole, if it was just a trifle larger."

While he was speaking he took his knife from his pocket, and attacked the putty with which one of the window-panes was secured. After a few quick passes it was all removed, and placing the blade of his knife beneath the glass, Featherweight forced it out of its place, and carefully laid it upon the chest. The opening thus made was not more than nine inches long and six wide, but it was large enough to admit the passage of Fred's little body, with some space to spare. After again reconnoitering the cabin, he thrust one of his legs through, then the other, and after a little squirming and some severe scratches from the sharp edges of the sash, he dropped down upon his feet. No sooner was he fairly landed than he ran to one of the stern windows of the cabin, threw it open, and without an instant's hesitation plunged into the water. But he did not strike out for the wharf as he had intended to do, for something caught his attention as he was descending through the air, and riveted his gaze. It was a large yacht, which was slowly passing up the harbor. He looked at her a moment, and then, with a cry of delight, swam toward her with all the speed he was capable of; but, before he had made a dozen strokes, a hoarse ejaculation from some one on the deck of the ship announced that he was discovered. He looked up, and saw the master of the vessel bending over the rail. "Good-bye, old fellow!" shouted Fred. "I've changed my mind. I'll not take passage with you this trip. If it is all the same to you I'll wait until the next."

For a moment the captain's astonishment was so great that he could neither move nor speak. He could not understand how his prisoner had effected his escape, after the care he had taken to secure him; and while he was thinking about it, Fred was improving every second of the time, and making astonishing headway through the water. The captain was not long in discovering this, and then he began to bustle about the deck in a state of great excitement.

"Avast there!" he cried. "Come back here, or I will wear a rope's end out on you." Then seeing that the swimmer paid no attention to his threat, he turned to his crew and ordered some of them to follow him into the yawl, which was made fast to the stern of the ship.

Fred heard the command and swam faster than

ever, stopping now and then, however, to raise himself as far as he could out of the water, and wave his hand toward the yacht. He tried to shout, but his excitement seemed to have taken away his voice, for he could not utter a syllable. But for all that he was seen, and his discovery seemed to produce no little commotion on the deck of the yacht. Several of her crew, led by a short, powerful-looking man, who wore a jaunty tarpaulin and wide collar, and carried a spy-glass in his hand, rushed to the rail; and the latter, after levelling his glass first at him and then at the ship, turned and issued some orders in a voice so loud and clear that Featherweight caught every word. There was no mistaking that voice or those shoulders, and neither was there any mistake possible in regard to the yacht, for there never was another like her. She was the Lookout; the man with the broad shoulders and stentorian voice was Uncle Dick; and of those who accompanied him to the side one was Fred's own father. The yacht at once changed her course and stood toward the fugitive, and the bustle on her deck and the rapid orders that were issued, told him that her boat was being manned. Would it arrive before the yawl that was now putting off from the ship?

Featherweight asked and answered this question in the same breath. As far as he was concerned it made no difference whether it did or not. His father had not followed him clear to Cuba to see another man make a prisoner of him, and as he was backed up by Uncle Dick and his crew, the matter could end in but one way.

"In bow!" commanded a stern voice behind him a few seconds later. "Parker, stand up, and fasten into his collar with the boat-hook."

The sharp, hissing sound which a boat makes when passing rapidly through the water, fell upon Fred's ear at this moment, and looking over his shoulder, he found the ship's yawl close upon him. He saw the bowman draw in his oar, and rise to his feet with the boat-hook in his hand, and an instant afterward his collar was drawn tight about his neck, his progress suddenly stopped, and then he was pulled back through the water and hauled into the yawl.

"I'll teach you to obey orders, my lad," said the captain, as he pushed Featherweight roughly down upon one of the thwarts. "I'll show you that a boy who comes aboard my vessel of his own free will, and ships for a voyage, and receives his advance fair and square, can't desert when he feels so inclined. You'll sup sorrow for this."

This remark was doubtless made for the benefit of the yawl's crew, none of whom were aware of the circumstances under which Fred had been brought on board the ship. The prisoner made no reply, but took his seat with the utmost composure, wiped the water from his face and looked toward the yacht. Her boat was just coming in sight around her stern. It was pulled by a sturdy crew, who bent to the oars as if they meant business. In the stern sheets sat Uncle Dick and Mr. Craven.

"I wonder what that schooner's boat is out for," said the captain, suddenly becoming aware that he was pursued.

"I suppose they saw me in the water, and thought they would pick me up," observed Featherweight.

"Well, you are picked up already, and they can go back and attend to their own business. You belong to me."

The captain said this in an indifferent tone, and settled back in his seat as if he had disposed of the matter; but it was plain that he was very much interested in the proceedings of the boat behind him. Now that the swimmer was picked up, he looked to see her turn back; but she did nothing of the kind. She came straight on in the wake of his yawl, and gained with every stroke of her crew. The captain's interest presently became uneasiness; and when at last the pursuing boat dashed up alongside, and her crew seized the gunwale of his yawl, his face was white with alarm. The instant the two boats touched, Fred was on his feet, and the next, his father's arms were about him. The captain heard the words "Father!" and "My son!" and then his under jaw dropped down, and his eyes seemed ready to start from their sockets. But he tried to keep up some show of courage and authority. "Hold on, there!" he exclaimed. "Hand that boy back here. He is one of my crew, who is trying to desert me."

"We happen to know a story worth two of that," said Uncle Dick, eying the captain until the latter quailed under his stern glance. "That boy is my friend's son. I'll trouble you to step into this boat."

"Is he, really?" said the captain, pretending not to hear Uncle Dick's order. "In that case I will let him off for a consideration."

"All the money you will receive for your share

in this business, has been paid to you by Mr. Bell, whom we shall have arrested in less than ten minutes. Step into this boat."

"What for?"

"Because we have use for you."

"And what if I don't choose to do it?"

"Then I shall take you up bodily and throw you in," said the old sailor, rising to his feet in just the right mood to carry his threat into execution.

"If you don't wish to suffer with your employer," said Mr. Craven, who was much calmer than any one else in Uncle Dick's boat, "you had better come with us peaceably."

The captain protested, and tried to assume a look of injured innocence, but it did not avail him. The two stern-looking men who were confronting him would not be denied, and Fred's jailer finally stepped into Uncle Dick's boat, and was carried on board the yacht, while his own crew, who had listened with wonder to all that passed, pulled back to the ship.

There were twenty men on board the Lookout, all old friends of Uncle Dick and Mr. Craven, who had volunteered to act as the crew, and assist in rescuing the prisoner if they overtook the smugglers, and these came forward in a body to welcome Fred as he sprang over the side. As he was handed about from one to another, hurried inquiries were made concerning the crew of the Banner, but Featherweight had no information to give. He had seen but two of them since his capture by the smugglers, and they had remained in sight scarcely more than five minutes. Where they went after they disappeared from his view, and what they did, he had no means of knowing.

"Never mind," said Uncle Dick. "We are after a gentleman who knows all about it; and we intend to make him tell, too."

The gentleman referred to was of course Mr. Bell. He saw the Lookout when she came into the harbor, and her appearance was all that was needed to show him that his affairs were getting into a desperate state. His game of deception was over now. He might prove more than a match for half a dozen inexperienced boys, but he knew that in the crew of the yacht, and especially in her commander and his brother, he would find his equals. He saw all that happened when Uncle Dick's boat came up with that of the captain of the ship; and when the latter gentleman was carried away a prisoner, and the yacht once more began to move up the harbor, directing her course toward the place where the Stella lay, he knew that it was high time he was bestirring himself. Without saying a word to any one, he jumped ashore, and made his way along the wharf. It was now dark, and although Mr. Bell could scarcely see or think of anything but the Lookout, he did not fail to discover something which made it clear to him that Uncle Dick and his friends had been wasting no time since they came into the harbor. It was a squad of soldiers who were marching quickly along the wharf, led by Mr. Gaylord, Mr. Chase, and a custom-house officer with whom he was well acquainted. As they had not seen him, Mr. Bell easily avoided them, and as soon as they passed, hurried through the gate and up the hill out of sight. Had he waited to see what they were going to do, he would have found that they boarded his vessel from one side, at the same moment that the crew of the Lookout came pouring over the other.

"Now, then, Mr. Officer," said Walter's father, as he sprang upon the Stella's deck, "here she is. Doesn't she look more like a smuggler than that little yacht? Hallo! Here's somebody who can tell us all about her," he added, seizing Fred's hand and shaking it so cordially, that the boy felt the effects of his gripe for half an hour afterward.

"I can show you where the arms and ammunition are," replied Featherweight, "and I suppose that's what you want to know. I am sorry to say that I can't tell you anything about Walter and the rest," he added, in reply to Mr. Gaylord's question. "Find Mr. Bell and Captain Conway, and make them tell."

At this moment, the master of the Stella appeared at the top of the companion ladder. Hearing the noise made by the boarding parties, he had come up to see what was the matter. One look must have been enough for him, for, without making a single inquiry, he turned and went down into his cabin again.

The first duty of the officer in command of the soldiers, was to direct that no one should be allowed to leave the vessel, and his second to accompany Fred Craven into the hold. Since the boy had last been there, the cargo had been broken out and stowed again, so as to conceal the secret hatchway; but Fred knew just where to find it, and there were men enough close at hand to remove the heavy boxes and hogsheads that covered it. In a very few minutes, a space was cleared in the middle of the hold, an axe was brought by one of the party, and the hatch forced up, disclosing to view the interior of the prison in which Fred had passed many a gloomy hour. The officer opened his eyes in surprise at the sight he beheld. He made an examination of the contents of a few of the boxes and bales, all of which were consigned to Don Casper Nevis, and then hurrying on deck, ordered every one of the crew of the Stella under arrest. The principal man, however, and the one he was most anxious to secure, was nowhere to be found. A thorough search of the town and the roads leading from it was at once ordered, all the crew of the Lookout volunteering to assist, except Uncle Dick and the other relatives of the missing boys, who went into the cabin to question Captain Conway. They were not as successful in their attempts to gain information as they had hoped to be. The captain, thoroughly cowed and anxious to propitiate his captors, answered all their inquiries as well as he could, and revealed to them the plans Mr. Bell had that afternoon put into operation. He knew that the Banner had been stolen by Pierre and the deserters, **who** intended **to go to** Havana in her, **but** he could not tell what **had** become of the boys. Chase and Wilson had been decoyed out to Don Casper's house by a note which they thought came from Walter, and **no** doubt they were still there. **Perhaps,** too, they knew where the rest of the missing crew could be found.

While the conversation was going on, the party in the cabin heard the roar of the guns of the fort, and saw the frigate get under way and leave the harbor. This was enough **to** put Uncle Dick and his friends **on** nettles. They **did not** want **to re-**remain there **inactive,** while the Banner was **in** danger (how greatly would their anxiety have been increased, had they known that Walter and his companions were in as much danger, at that moment, as those who stole their vessel), but their crew were all ashore looking for Mr. Bell, and so was the custom-house officer, and they were obliged to await their return. At the end of an hour, their suspense was relieved by the arrival of the official and some of the Lookout's company. Their search had been successful—the fugitive leader of the smugglers having been overtaken and captured while on his **way to** Don Casper's house. The officers had pumped him most effectually, and learning that he had been deceived as to the character of the Banner, and that the precautions he had taken to prevent her leaving the port, would most likely insure her destruction, he was anxious to do all in his power to save her. He readily complied with Uncle Dick's request to sail with him in pursuit of the frigate, and greatly relieved the fears of Mr. Chase, by assuring him that what he had heard from Mr. Bell, made him confident that his son would be found at Don Casper's.

The rescued boy was the hero of the hour. While the Lookout was flying over the Gulf toward the bay at the rear of the Don's plantation, he was entertaining a group of eager listeners by recounting the various exciting events that had happened since the day of the "Wild Hog Hunt." But it was not long before he was obliged to give place to those who had adventures more exciting than his own to relate. The officer of the deck, whom Uncle Dick had instructed to keep a lookout for the frigate, came down to report that there were lights ahead: and that, although but a short distance away, they had only just appeared in view—a fact which, according to his way of thinking, proved something.

"It does, indeed," said the custom-house officer. "Why should a vessel be under way on such a night as this without showing lights? She's another smuggler. Captain, you will oblige me by going as close to her as you can."

If the approaching vessel was engaged in honest business she was certainly acting in a very suspicious manner. So thought Uncle Dick, after he had watched her lights for a few minutes. She stood first on one tack, and then on the other, as if trying to dodge the Lookout, and this made the old sailor all the more determined that she should not do it. He kept his vessel headed as straight for her as she could go; the custom-house official stood by, rubbing his hands in great glee, and telling himself that another smuggler's course was almost run; and the crew leaned over the rail, straining their eyes through the darkness, and waiting impatiently to obtain the first glimpse of the stranger. She came into view at last---a modest-looking little craft, with two boys perched upon the main cross-trees, busy with a broken topmast. The old sailor and his brother started as if they had been shot, and the former seizing his trumpet, sprang upon the rail, steadying himself by the fore shrouds. "Walter!" he yelled.

"Uncle Dick!" came the answer, after a moment's pause, in surprised and joyous accents.

After this there was a long silence. Walter, having answered the hail, had not another word to say, and neither had the Lookout's commander or any of his crew, whose amazement and delight were too great for utterance. They seemed unable to remove their eyes from the little yacht. What adventures had she passed through since they last saw her? She had sailed hundreds of miles over a stormy gulf to a country that none of her crew had ever visited before, had been shot at by the heavy guns of the fort, chased by a frigate, and stolen by deserters, and there she was, looking little the worse for her rough experience. At length Uncle Dick's voice broke the silence. "Are you all safe?" he inquired.

He asked this question in a trembling voice, grasping the shrouds with a firmer hold, and bending forward a little as if to meet a shock from some invisible source, while his crew held their breath, and listened eagerly for the reply.

"Yes, sir; all except Chase. He is not with us He must be at Don Casper's."

"Thank Heaven!" was the involuntary ejaculation of everyone of the Lookout's company. "To go through so much and come out with the loss of only one of the crew, who may yet be found alive and well! It is wonderful!"

Uncle Dick's face wore an expression that no one had ever seen there before, and his voice was husky as he seized his brother's hand, and wringing it energetically, asked what was to be done now? Mr. Gaylord and the officer advised an immediate return to Don Casper's; and in obedience to Uncle Dick's orders, the Lookout again filled away, and the Banner came about, and followed in her wake.

The adventures we have attempted to describe in this volume comprise all the exciting events in the history of the Club's short sojourn in Cuba, but by no means all the interesting ones. If time would permit, we might enter into minute details concerning the grand re-union that took place in the cabin of the Lookout shortly after she and the Banner entered the bay, and anchored at the stern of the frigate. It was a happy meeting, in spite of the gloom thrown over it by the absence of Chase, and the consequent anxiety and distress of his father. Wilson was obliged to tell, over and over again, all he knew about the missing boy. He held his auditors spell-bound for half an hour, and when he finished his story, Walter began. Among the listeners was the captain of the iron-clad; and when the young commander told how narrowly he had escaped discovery and capture when the man-of-war was entering the bay, the officer patted him on the head and said that he was a brave lad and a good sailor.

Uncle Dick and his crew were highly indignant over what had happened in the cove at Lost Island. They had heard it all from the master of the revenue cutter. The old sailor and his brother, who, it will be remembered, were in the woods searching for Featherweight when the Banner began her cruise, returned home at daylight, and learning from Mrs. Gaylord where the boys had gone, they hurried to Bellville, raised a crew for the Lookout, and put to sea. Before they had gone far they found the John Basset, drifting helplessly about on the waves, her engine being disabled. That explained why she did not make her appearance at Lost Island

Uncle Dick took Mr. Chase and Mr. Craven aboard his own vessel, listened in amazement to their story, and shortly afterward met the cutter. He held a long consultation with her captain, who, after describing what had taken place in the cove, told him that the last he saw of the Banner she was following after the Stella, which had set sail for Cuba. Uncle Dick at once filled away in pursuit; but being too old to believe that a vessel carrying contraband goods would go to so large a port as Havana, ran down until land was sighted, and then held along the coast, carefully examining every bay and inlet. As the Lookout was a much swifter vessel than the Stella, he gained time enough to do all this work, and to reach Port Platte on the evening of the same day the smuggler arrived there.

Mutual explanations being ended, the entire party, accompanied by a squad from the frigate, went ashore to look for Chase. They searched high and low (the Club found time to peep into the wine cellar where he and Wilson had been confined), but could find nothing of him. At daylight the three vessels sailed in company for Port Platte, and the whole of that day and the succeeding one was spent in fruitless search. Chase had disappeared as utterly as if he had never had an existence. Being satisfied at last that he had shipped on board some vessel bound for the States, his father consented to sail with his friends for Bellville. They reached the village without any mishap, and in ample season for the Club to perfect numerous plans for their amusement during the holidays. Some interesting events happened about that time— one especially which threw our heroes into ecstacies —and what they were, shall be told in " THE SPORTSMAN'S CLUB AMONG THE TRAPPERS."

THE END.